Exploring
Christianity

WITHDRAWN

The Bible and Christian Belief

Gwyneth Windsor
and John Hughes

HEINEMANN
EDUCATIONAL

Heinemann Educational,
a division of Heinemann Educational Books Ltd,
Halley Court, Jordan Hill, Oxford OX2 8EJ

OXFORD   LONDON   EDINBURGH
MELBOURNE   SYDNEY   AUCKLAND
IBADAN   NAIROBI   GABORONE   HARARE
KINGSTON   PORTSMOUTH N H   (USA)
SINGAPORE   MADRID   BOLOGNA   ATHENS

First published 1990

British Library Cataloguing in Publication Data
Windsor, Gwyneth
   The Bible and Christian belief.
1. Christianity
I. Title   II. Hughes, John   III. Series
   200

ISBN 0 435 30271 X

Designed and produced by VAP Publishing Services, Kidlington, Oxon

Printed and bound in Spain by Mateu Cromo

Acknowledgements
Thanks are due to Religious Studies Consultant W. Owen Cole, Roger Owen and Janey Graham for commenting on the manuscript.

The publishers would like to thank the following for permission to reproduce photographs: J. C. Allen pp. 57 (bottom), 84 (D); Ancient Art and Architecture Collection/Ronald Sheridan pp. 4, 7, 8, 18, 40 (B), 41; Andes Press Agency/Carlos Reyes pp. 20 (B), 22, 48 (A), 57 (top), 72 (A), 74 (G), 76, 80 (top), 81 (bottom left), 82 (C and D), 83 (D and E), 85 (F); The Anglican Consultative Council pp. 32 (C), 84 (A), 85 (E); Baptist Union p. 66 (E); Barnaby's Picture Library pp. 21 (right), 30 (E); Eric Bouvet/Gamma/Frank Spooner Pictures p. 15; Bridgeman Art Library p. 74 (I); Camera Press pp. 31 (G), 62 (C); Camera Press/Fotokronika Tass p. 51 (F); Thierry Campion/Gamma/Frank Spooner Pictures p. 77 (C); J. Allan Cash Ltd pp. 5, 18 (B) 26 (E and F), 32 (B), 40 (A), 68 (B); Church's Ministry Among the Jews p. 34; Colorific p. 25 (C); The Controller of Her Majesty's Stationery Office p. 35; Karim Daher/Gamma/Frank Spooner Pictures p. 73 (C); Keith Ellis Collection pp. 59 (E), 89 (B); Greg Evans Photo Library pp. 64 (B), 66 (D); Gamma/Frank Spooner Pictures p. 25 (B); Melanie Friend/Format p. 62 (D); Glasgow Museums and Art Galleries p. 53 (D); Sally and Richard Greenhill pp. 21 (left), 29, 49; Sonia Halliday Photographs pp. 9 (C), 18 (J), 27, 28 (A and B), 33, 59 (D), 60, 64 (A), 68 (A), 69, 74 (E and F); Sonia Halliday Photographs/F.H.C. Birch pp. 61, 72 (B), 77 (B and D), 84 (C); Robert Harding Picture Library pp. 20 (A), 24, 43 (bottom), 65; Hutchison Library pp. 55, 86; Hutchison/B. Moser/Granada TV p. 92 (A); ITC Entertainment Ltd. pp. 30 (D), 31 (H), 36 (A and B), 52 (A and B), 53 (C), 56 (A and B); Knight and Hunt photo/Zefa p. 43 (top); Ansin Liaison/Gamma/Frank Spooner Pictures p. 84 (B); F. Lochon/Gamma/Frank Spooner Pictures p. 92 (C); Martin Mayer/Network p. 10 (E); Oxfam p. 81 (top); Brenda Prince/Format p. 80 (A); John Rylands University Library of Manchester p. 9 (B); The Salvation Army pp. 48 (C), 81 (bottom right); Clifford Shirley p. 91; Vladimir Sichov/Rex Features pp. 48 (B), 95 (E and F); John Sturrock/Network pp. 47, 51 (top); Topham Picture Library pp. 30 (F), 50, 90; Jerry Wooldridge/Stanley Thornes p. 73 (D); Alan Woolfitt/Susan Griggs Agency p. 89 (A); World Council of Churches/Peter Williams p. 92 (B); Zefa Picture Library (UK) Ltd. p. 26 (D).

All other photographs supplied by the authors.

Cover photograph by Zefa Picture Library (UK) Ltd.

CONTENTS

WHAT KIND OF BOOK IS IT?

Some people find the Bible quite confusing. They pick it up, and expect it to be just one book. In fact, it is like having a complete library. There are 66 books altogether, and they are divided into two main sections. The first of these is called the Old Testament. There are 39 books in this part of the Bible. The second part is called the New Testament, and there are 27 books in this part.

It's not all the same kind of writing either. Some parts are history, and there are some very exciting stories! Some parts are poetry. There are collections of laws, as well as sayings of important people called **prophets**.

Look carefully at the picture of the Bible bookshop on this page to help you to see all the different kinds of writing which you find in the Bible.

Some parts of the Bible are very ancient indeed, and no-one really knows

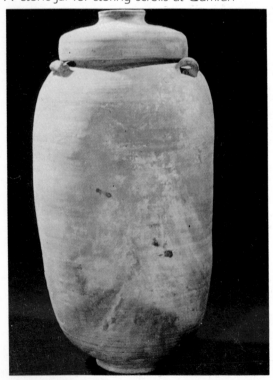

A Stone jar for storing scrolls at Qumran

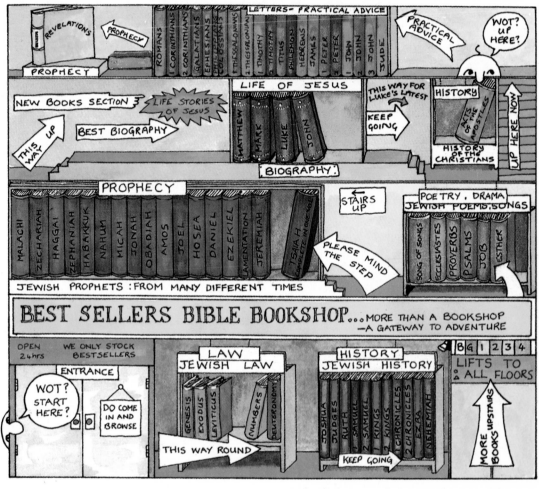

when some parts of it were first written down – it could be as long ago as nearly four thousand years. The latest parts to be written down date from the time of the **Roman Empire**.

The word 'Bible' comes from a Greek word 'biblios', which means 'book'. Of course, the Bible didn't look like a book at first, because books weren't invented when it was written. It would originally have been a series of scrolls, one for each book. Isaiah usually took three scrolls because it is so long! Look at the picture of the stone jars which were used for keeping the scrolls. The ones in the picture were found at a place called Qumran, near the Dead Sea. The famous **Dead Sea Scrolls** were kept in these jars. These are the earliest copies which we have of parts of the Old Testament. They were found in 1947, and they help

us to prove that the words of the Bible had not changed in any important way through being copied out by hand for hundreds of years.

The Old Testament was written originally in Hebrew. This is the language spoken by the people of Israel in the Bible. It is still spoken by Israeli people (**Jews**) now. Later on, the Old Testament was translated into Greek.

The New Testament was written originally in Greek. Later on, both the Old Testament and the New Testament were translated into Latin. From the sixteenth century onwards, the Bible has been translated into most of the languages of the world.

The Old Testament begins with the story of Creation. Then there is the history of the people of Israel, later called the Jews, from the time of Abraham onwards. It looks forward to a time when God will send a special person to help people to behave the way God wants them to. This special person is called the **Messiah**.

Christians believe that Jesus of Nazareth was this special person. The New Testament is about his life, and about the people who began to follow him and to tell the world about him.

NOTES/DATABASE

Use the glossary to look up the meanings of the following words. Then use the definitions to make your own notes or suitable entries on your database.

Prophets   Jew

Roman Empire   Messiah

Dead Sea Scrolls

This is what Hebrew looks like:

GENESIS. בראשית

1 בְּרֵאשִׁ֖ית בָּרָ֣א אֱלֹהִ֑ים אֵ֥ת הַשָּׁמַ֖יִם וְאֵ֥ת הָאָֽרֶץ׃ וְהָאָ֗רֶץ הָיְתָ֥ה תֹ֨הוּ֙ וָבֹ֔הוּ וְחֹ֖שֶׁךְ עַל־פְּנֵ֣י תְה֑וֹם וְר֣וּחַ אֱלֹהִ֔ים מְרַחֶ֖פֶת עַל־פְּנֵ֥י הַמָּֽיִם׃ וַיֹּ֥אמֶר אֱלֹהִ֖ים יְהִ֣י א֑וֹר וַֽיְהִי־אֽוֹר׃ וַיַּ֧רְא אֱלֹהִ֛ים אֶת־הָא֖וֹר כִּי־ט֑וֹב וַיַּבְדֵּ֣ל אֱלֹהִ֔ים בֵּ֥ין הָא֖וֹר וּבֵ֥ין הַחֹֽשֶׁךְ׃ וַיִּקְרָ֨א אֱלֹהִ֤ים ׀ לָאוֹר֙ י֔וֹם וְלַחֹ֖שֶׁךְ קָ֣רָא לָ֑יְלָה וַֽיְהִי־עֶ֥רֶב וַֽיְהִי־בֹ֖קֶר י֥וֹם אֶחָֽד׃ פ וַיֹּ֣אמֶר אֱלֹהִ֔ים יְהִ֥י רָקִ֖יעַ בְּת֣וֹךְ הַמָּ֑יִם וִיהִ֣י מַבְדִּ֔יל בֵּ֥ין מַ֖יִם לָמָֽיִם׃ וַיַּ֣עַשׂ אֱלֹהִים֮ אֶת־הָרָקִיעַ֒ וַיַּבְדֵּ֗ל בֵּ֤ין הַמַּ֨יִם֙ אֲשֶׁר֙ מִתַּ֣חַת לָרָקִ֔יעַ וּבֵ֣ין הַמַּ֔יִם אֲשֶׁ֖ר מֵעַ֣ל לָרָקִ֑יעַ וַֽיְהִי־כֵֽן׃ וַיִּקְרָ֧א אֱלֹהִ֛ים לָֽרָקִ֖יעַ שָׁמָ֑יִם וַֽיְהִי־עֶ֥רֶב וַֽיְהִי־בֹ֖קֶר י֥וֹם שֵׁנִֽי׃ פ וַיֹּ֣אמֶר אֱלֹהִ֗ים יִקָּו֣וּ הַמַּ֨יִם

This is what Greek looks like:

ΚΑΤΑ ΙΩΑΝΝΗΝ

ΕΝ ἀρχῇ ἦν ὁ Λόγος, καὶ ὁ Λόγος ἦν πρὸς τὸν
2 Θεόν, καὶ Θεὸς ἦν ὁ Λόγος.   Οὗτος ἦν ἐν
3 ἀρχῇ πρὸς τὸν Θεόν. πάντα δι᾽ αὐτοῦ ἐγένετο,
4 καὶ χωρὶς αὐτοῦ ἐγένετο οὐδὲ ἕν. ὃ γέγονεν | ἐν
αὐτῷ ζωὴ ἦν, καὶ ἡ ζωὴ ἦν τὸ φῶς τῶν ἀνθρώ-
5 πων. καὶ τὸ φῶς ἐν τῇ σκοτίᾳ φαίνει, καὶ ἡ σκοτία
6 αὐτὸ οὐ κατέλαβεν.   Ἐγένετο ἄνθρωπος,
ἀπεσταλμένος παρὰ Θεοῦ, ὄνομα αὐτῷ Ἰωάννης·
7 οὗτος ἦλθεν εἰς μαρτυρίαν, ἵνα μαρτυρήσῃ περὶ

ACTIVITIES

1 Quick quiz

Answer the following questions in complete sentences.

a What are the two parts of the Bible usually called?

b How many books are there altogether?

c Look carefully at the diagram of the Bible bookshop to find out what different kinds of writing there are in the Bible. Make a list which shows what you have found out.

d When was the latest part of the Bible written down?

e What does the word 'Bible' mean?

f What would the books of the Bible have been written on at first?

g What do the Dead Sea Scrolls help us to prove?

h What language was the Old Testament written down in originally?

i What language was the New Testament written down in originally?

j Write two sentences to say what the Old Testament is about.

k Write one sentence which says what the New Testament is about.

B Hebrew advertising

2 Learn some Hebrew

Turn to the person sitting next to you and say 'shalom'. This means 'peace' and is the usual way of saying 'hello' in the Bible and in Israel today. The polite answer is 'shalom aleichem' – 'peace to you'

Try it! Don't be embarrassed.

This is how it looks in Hebrew:

שלום אלכם

Copy it into your book and write down the meaning. Hebrew is written from right to left, so be careful not to smudge your work!

FURTHER ACTIVITIES

1 Look carefully at the Bible bookshop on page 4.

a Either (i) Make a model of the Bible bookshop using matchboxes. Then use a Bible dictionary to find out about each book, and place a slip of paper in each matchbox saying what it is about. You can decorate each matchbox book too.

Or (ii) Draw a picture of how the Bible library might have looked at Qumran.

> The librarian at Alexandria was asked to put the Bible in his library. He couldn't find a way of classifying it because it has so many different kinds of books in it.

b Using the diagram of the Bible bookshop, copy and complete the following chart about the Old Testament. You will need to put each book in the correct column.

Law	Writings (poetry)	History	Prophets

c Now use the diagram of the Bible bookshop to complete the chart shown below about the New Testament. Once again, you will need to put each book in the correct column.

Lives of Jesus (Gospels)	History	Letters	Prophecy

2 Design your own front covers for the Old Testament (The Bible I) and then the New Testament (The Bible II).

Here are some suggestions to help you:

ARCHAEOLOGICAL EXTRA

A small boy, climbing around the mountains near the Dead Sea, may be responsible for one of the greatest archaeological finds of the century. *1947*

THE DEAD SEA SCROLLS . . . THE MOST EXCITING FIND THIS CENTURY!

Whilst looking for his sheep and goats, a young Arab boy climbed the hillside near Jericho, at a spot known as Qumran. During the search for his animals he wandered into a cave where he made the most amazing find! There were a large number of stone pots which had been used to store scrolls. These scrolls would have deteriorated so rapidly

in the desert near the salt-laden Dead Sea that people used stone jars to store them — a kind of ancient library. These scrolls seem to date from well before the time of Jesus. They are in Hebrew and are parts of the Old Testament. If proved to be genuine, they will be the oldest known copies of the Old Testament.

Scholars who have examined the scrolls say that they are identical to the usual text of the Old Testament. This proves how reliable the scribes were who copied out the manuscripts over the years. These scrolls are 700 years older than the oldest ones previously known. There are ten caves at Qumran. Archaeologists hope for more finds when they search the rest of the caves.

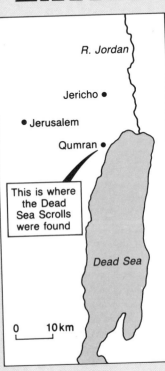

R. Jordan

Jericho ●

● Jerusalem

Qumran ●

This is where the Dead Sea Scrolls were found

Dead Sea

0   10km

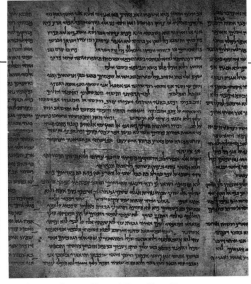

C One of the Dead Sea Scrolls

3 Things to do

a Look at the picture of the scroll. Now make a model of a scroll. Copy the words of Deuteronomy 6:4,5 onto your scroll. This is the most important Jewish Law.

b Imagine you are a newspaper reporter trying to get an exclusive interview with the boy who found the Dead Sea Scrolls.
  (i) What questions do you think you need to ask?
  (ii) What answers do you think he will give?

c Now answer these questions, using the Archaeological Extra to help you:
  (i) How did the boy make the find?
  (ii) Where were the scrolls stored?
  (iii) Why were they stored like this?
  (iv) When do archaeologists think these scrolls were written?
  (v) Why are the scrolls so important?
  (vi) Where else do you think archaeologists will search?

ONE OF THE EXCITING STORIES

To find this exciting story turn to the Book of Jonah.

4 Look up the Bible verse under each picture, and write your own captions. The pictures do not tell the complete story. Write down what happened next.

Now, answer these questions:

5 a What did Jonah do when God told him to preach in the city of Nineveh?
  b What happened on the ship?
  c Why was Jonah thrown into the sea?
  d How long was he in the big fish?
  e What did Jonah do while he was in the big fish?
  f Why was the fish sick?
  g What did Jonah do then?
  h What rather peculiar thing did the King of Nineveh do?
  i Was God pleased?
  j Was Jonah pleased?
  k How did God show Jonah what he meant?

The Old Testament was the first part of the Bible to be translated from Hebrew into another language. By the third century BCE (Before the Common Era), there were many Jews living in countries around the Mediterranean as well as in Israel. Many of these spoke Greek. It was therefore important to them that they should be able to read their **Scriptures** (the word they often used for the Old Testament) in the language they spoke best. So in Alexandria, in the third century BCE, a translation of the Old Testament was made from Hebrew into Greek. This Greek version was the one which the early Christians used.

Jesus would have known Hebrew, but the everyday language he spoke was **Aramaic**. He possibly knew some Greek as well, because that was the usual language of the Eastern Mediterranean at the time. When the **disciples** began to tell people about Jesus outside Israel, they had to tell them in Greek, because that was the language most people spoke. So it is not surprising that the biographies of Jesus, which we call the **Gospels** (the word means 'good news'), were first written down in Greek.

The oldest fragment (small piece) of the Gospels which we have was written in Greek. It dates from about 130 CE (Common Era). It is a part of St John's Gospel. It is part of the page of a book (the writing is on both sides) rather than a scroll (the writing on a scroll is on one side only). Some people believe that books were actually invented so that people could pass around copies of the Gospels more easily. It also saved **papyrus** or **vellum**, the two materials used for writing on. So many people wanted to read about the life of Jesus that very soon there were lots of copies of the four Gospels in existence. Two of the very old ones which we still have are:

Codex Sinaiaticus
Codex Vaticanus

PUTTING THE BIBLE IN OUR LANGUAGE

1 From Greek to Latin!

2 We need the Bible in Latin because in Rome, that's the language we all speak.

3

4 But it didn't all happen over night . . .

5 It was like this:

6 They really didn't understand Greek – well, they lived in Rome and Western Europe where many people spoke Latin.

7 So in the fourth century a monk called Jerome decided to translate the Bible into Latin – to help more people to understand it.

A Codex Sinaiaticus

Some **monks**, who did not realize its value, were burning this old **manuscript** at the **Monastery** of St Katherine on the Sinai peninsula. Visitors to the monastery were able to stop them and rescue the ancient book. The word 'codex' is a Latin word to describe a book.

In 70 CE Jerusalem was destroyed. Rome became the most important city for Christians instead of Jerusalem. Soon most Christians in the Western Mediterranean spoke Latin instead of Greek. They did not understand the Greek which the Bible was written in, so a monk called Jerome translated the Bible into Latin so that people would be able to read it in their own language.

Throughout the time we call the Middle Ages, all educated people spoke Latin. Most ordinary people could not read. Books were very expensive because they all had to be copied out by hand. All the church services were in Latin as well.

At the end of the fifteenth century printing was invented. This meant that books became much cheaper. Ordinary people could now afford to buy books. Learning to read became very popular. One of the first books to be printed was the Latin version of the Bible.

Soon people wanted the Bible in their own languages so that they could read it and understand it for themselves. On the next few pages, you will find out about some of the people who made it possible for the Bible to be in ordinary languages such as English and German instead of in Latin. Some of these people were tortured, and some even died for their belief that it was important for people to be able to understand the Bible easily. This is what a man called Erasmus said in 1520:

"I want every boy who ploughs a field to be able to read the Bible, whatever language he speaks!"

> WOT NEXT?
> I DON'T SPEAK LATIN
> DO I?

NOTES/DATABASE

Use the glossary to look up the meanings of the following words. Then use the definitions to write your own notes or suitable entries on your database.

Scriptures	Vellum
Aramaic	Codex
Disciple	Monk
Gospel	Manuscript
Papyrus	Monastery

B Muratorian fragment – the earliest Greek version of John's Gospel in existence

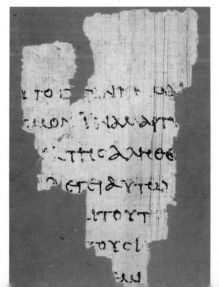

ACTIVITIES

1 Quick quiz

a Which part of the Bible was translated first?

b Why was it important to translate the Old Testament into Greek?

c What language did Jesus speak?

d What was the usual language of the Eastern Mediterranean countries?

e What is the special word for the biographies of Jesus which are in the Bible?

f Why is it important that the oldest fragment of St John's Gospel is written on both sides of the page?

g Why do some people think that books were invented?

h What is a Codex?

i Why did Rome become the most important city for Christians?

j Why was the Bible translated into Latin?

k Why were books very expensive in the Middle Ages?

l Which invention made it possible for ordinary people to buy books?

m Why do you think learning to read became popular?

n Why do you think the Bible was one of the first books to be printed?

o Why do you think Erasmus wanted everyone to be able to read the Bible in their own language?

2 a Why do you think it was necessary to translate the Bible from Greek into Latin?

b Find the names of some other books written in Latin.

c Many of our English words come from Latin words. Try to guess the meanings of the Latin words in Column A in the chart below. Copy the chart, and write your guesses in Column B.

A	B
remotus	remote
theatrum	
circus	
angelus	
transfero	
medicina	
censor	
conductor	

C A handwritten Latin Bible

FURTHER ACTIVITIES

ADVERTISEMENT FEATURE

NEW INVENTION WILL CHANGE THE WORLD!

Those of us involved with this fantastic new invention will not think this claim is exaggerated. We believe that printing, instead of copying books etc. by hand, will change every aspect of life. BUSINESS will be changed! Shopkeepers and other business owners will be able to keep accurate records of their businesses. They will all learn to read. In a few years, everyone will be able to understand these strange scratchings on paper, which are words.

It is a quicker way of passing on information about new inventions! Printed information about new inventions will soon be sent to lots of different addresses. It will be a revolution in communication. Printed copies of designs, pictures and ideas can be passed on!

D Fifteenth century printing press

E Modern newspapers rolling off printing presses

People will be able to read the Bible in their own language — because soon everyone will be able to read. Prices of books will drop and everyone will be able to afford them.

Don't be left behind! Soon all jobs will require people who can read. Learn soon, teach others. Pass on this vital information.

Break the power of the Church by finding out what the Bible really says! Soon there will be translations in YOUR language!

POSSIBLY THE BIGGEST REVOLUTION THE WORLD WILL EVER KNOW!

1 The above advertising handout could have been the kind of thing people were saying about the invention of printing.

a Make a list of the changes there would be as more and more people could read.

b Why do you think the Bible was one of the first books ever to be printed?

c Why do you think the invention of printing helped to make people want to read the Bible in their own languages?

The same kind of thing could be written now about technology.

d Rewrite the above advertisement referring to technology in the present day instead of the invention of printing.
Make sure you include ideas about how technology can help people understand more about the Bible.

William Tyndale
1492 – 1536

CUSTOMS NOTICE

It is illegal to import Bibles in English into England. It is dangerous, and is banned in any language people understand.

Customs officers have today seized a large consignment of Bibles in English from a ship in Dover harbour. It is believed these were destined for the Black Market. They are reputed to have a street value of £2000. Customs officers are interviewing three crew members accused of smuggling Bibles.

BIBLE BONFIRE IN LONDON – 1526

Bishops have bought up the English Bibles of William Tyndale and today had a bonfire! They burned all these illegal documents in front of St Paul's Cathedral. A spokesman for the bishops said, "We hope this will be the last we hear about this treacherous nonsense of suggesting that the Bible should be in English. It is very dangerous to let ordinary people understand the Bible."
What will Tyndale do NEXT?

ILLEGAL BIBLES BEING PRINTED AGAIN – 1530

Tyndale is reported to be back at work printing illegal English Bibles. He is probably at Cologne in Germany.

TYNDALE ARRESTED! – 1536

William Tyndale, the Bible smuggler, has been arrested in Antwerp.

539 **All churches must have an English Bible, by order, the King of England**

2 **The story of William Tyndale is an exciting one.**
Use a Church history database or books to find out as much as you can about him.

His life story would make an interesting video.

People you will need:

a script writers

b actors

c director

d stage manager

e graphic designers

f film crew.

Some people might like to design advertisements and a sleeve for your video. If you have a computer with a desktop publishing system, you could use this to produce your advertising material.

You may also like to appoint reporters for the 'premier'. They will then need to write reviews of the video (for different newspapers, of course). These could also be printed on the desktop publishing system.

If you have a video digitiser, you could also digitise some pictures from the video to include in your reviews and advertisements.

F Bibles ready to smuggle into England, 1525

3 **There are people who smuggle Bibles into Communist countries, even today.**
One of them is called Brother Andrew. You can find out about him by referring to the booklet *Bible Smuggler* by David Wallington (RMEP).

Now answer these questions:

a Why did Tyndale need to smuggle Bibles?

b Why do you think he wanted to make sure people could read the Bible in their own language?

c Do you think the government should have laws about what people can read? Give reasons for your answer.

d Why do you think Brother Andrew smuggled Bibles into Communist countries?

4 **In groups:**

a Discuss, then write down the reasons why you think the Communist authorities have opposed Bibles.

b Many of the people in governments who ban Bibles have possibly never read one.

Do you think it is right to ban something or to speak against it without ever having read it? Give some reasons for your answer.

G "Lord, open the King of England's eyes."

Jews divide the Old Testament into three main sections:

1 Torah, or Law
2 Nevi'im or Prophets
3 Ketuvim, or Writings.

Most English versions are in the same order as the Hebrew Bible. The Roman Catholic translation, which is called the Jerusalem Bible, has a different order because it follows the same order as the Greek version which was called the Septuagint.

It is a bit easier, in fact, to think of the Old Testament as being divided into four main sections:

1 The Law (or **Pentateuch**, the first five books of the Bible)
2 The History books
3 Prophecy
4 Poetry.

Look back to page 4 where there is a plan of a Bible bookshop. This will help you sort out which books belong in each section.

At first, the stories in the early part of the Old Testament were not written down. They were passed on, word for word, and from generation to generation. Imagine some ancient Bedouins, sitting in their tents under the stars, telling the stories of their ancestors.

After a while, these stories were written down. They were probably written on clay tablets. Archaeologists have found many clay tablets which date from Old Testament times. Later still, they were written on **scrolls**, which looked very much the same as those used in Jewish worship today.

The people of Israel have always believed in a God who leads and guides his people in a very real way. The history of the Jewish people is very important to them because it is a history of how God has led and guided them for many centuries. It is not surprising to discover that the Jews were amongst the first people to start writing history. Other

AT FIRST THE OLD STORIES ABOUT GOD WERE TOLD AROUND THE CAMP-FIRE AT NIGHT. THEY WERE REPEATED WORD FOR WORD. (This is called ORAL TRADITION.)

THEN THEY LEARNED TO WRITE.

SO THEY WROTE STORIES ON CLAY TABLETS. (These were a bit heavy to carry around.)

HEBREW

LATER ON THEY WROTE ON SCROLLS

Help! I only speak Greek!

THEY BEGAN TO NEED A GREEK VERSION

So 70 men got together to translate the Old Testament into Greek. THIS IS CALLED THE "SEPTUAGINT" OR "LXX" FOR SHORT!

GREEK

I'm a Greek speaking Jew. I read the Septuagint.

MOST CHRISTIANS AT FIRST USED THE LXX

Εν αρχη ην ο λογος

HEBREW

I'm a Hebrew speaking Jew. I read the Scriptures in Hebrew.

nations wrote lists of events and of reigns of kings – the Jews wrote down details of what happened. Their history is part of their faith. The marvellous things which had happened to them became real proof that their God led them, guided them and cared for them.

The most important event in the history of Israel was when God led the Israelites out of Egypt. They had all been slaves in the land of Egypt. God used Moses to lead the people of Israel into the land of **Canaan**, which is now called Israel. They called Canaan 'the **Promised Land**'. It was the land which God had promised to Abraham

(Genesis 12:1–4). Even now, Jews remember this event. Every year there is a festival called **Passover**. This celebrates the night when the Israelites left Egypt. Every Jew is supposed to treat the **Exodus**, as we call this event, as if it had happened to him or her personally.

The Books of Joshua and Judges record the time when the Israelites were fighting for the land of Israel and settling in it. When kings were appointed, the lives of the kings and the most important events of their reigns were written down. The Old Testament is a very honest book. If someone was a good king, it praises them. If someone was a bad king it says so quite clearly.

There were times when Israel did not do what God wanted. The Old Testament tells us about the **prophets** who spoke out. They told all the people, including the King, that they needed to change their way of life.

The Old Testament stops several hundred years before the birth of Jesus. Nothing more was added to it, although there are some books in the **Apocrypha** which were written nearer to the time of Jesus. These provide valuable historical information. By 90 CE the Old Testament was complete. Christians were already making a list of the books of the New Testament. The Jews held a council at Jamnia in 90 CE at which they made a list of books which they thought to be holy. These are called '**scriptures**'. They are important to Jews as a record of the way God has led and guided them.

Christians can learn more about God, and about Jesus, from the Old Testament. **Muslims** also share the same history. The Bible is the only holy book in the world which is important to people of three religions. Each of these religions worships the one God of the Old Testament.

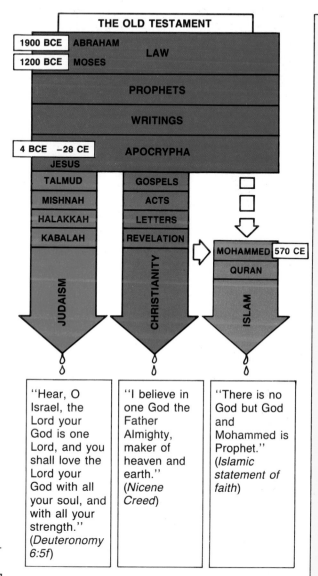

THE OLD TESTAMENT

1900 BCE ABRAHAM — LAW — 1200 BCE MOSES

PROPHETS

WRITINGS

4 BCE –28 CE APOCRYPHA / JESUS

TALMUD	GOSPELS
MISHNAH	ACTS
HALAKKAH	LETTERS
KABALAH	REVELATION

JUDAISM — CHRISTIANITY — MOHAMMED 570 CE / QURAN — ISLAM

"Hear, O Israel, the Lord your God is one Lord, and you shall love the Lord your God with all your soul, and with all your strength." (*Deuteronomy 6:5f*)

"I believe in one God the Father Almighty, maker of heaven and earth." (*Nicene Creed*)

"There is no God but God and Mohammed is Prophet." (*Islamic statement of faith*)

NOTES/DATABASE

Use the glossary to look up the meanings of the following words. Then use the definitions to make your own notes or suitable entries on your database.

Pentateuch	Exodus
Scroll	Prophet
Canaan	Apocrypha
Promised Land	Scriptures
Passover	Muslim

ACTIVITIES

1 **Discuss**
What is similar about what Judaism, Christianity and Islam believe about God?

2 **Quick quiz**
a What are the names of the three main sections into which the Jews divide the Old Testament?

b Make a list of the four sections in which it is easiest to think of the Old Testament.

c What is the modern Roman Catholic translation of the Bible called?

d How were the stories in the Old Testament passed on from generation to generation before they were written down?

e What have archaeologists found which has helped them to discover how the Bible was originally written?

f Why is history so important to the Jewish people?

g Other nations wrote lists of events and the reigns of kings. In what way was this different from how the Jews recorded their history?

h Describe the most important event in the history of ancient Israel.

i Which Jewish festival celebrates this event?

j Which two books of the Bible record the struggle for the land of Israel?

k Why is the Old Testament thought to be a very honest book?

l What happened when Israel did not do what God wanted?

m Where would you look for valuable historical information about the Jews just before the birth of Jesus?

n Why was the Council of Jamnia important?

o For which three religions is the Old Testament important?

FURTHER ACTIVITIES

1 Family tree

One of the ways people got interested in history was by looking at their family trees. Look at the family tree below which is taken from the Old Testament, and answer the questions.

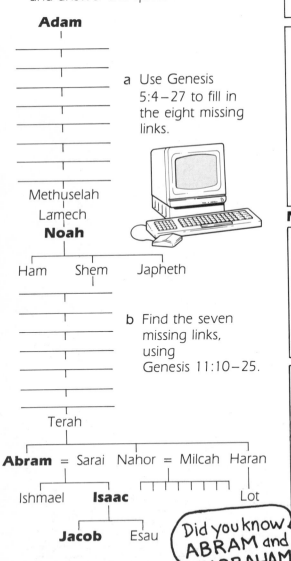

Adam

a Use Genesis 5:4–27 to fill in the eight missing links.

Methuselah
Lamech
Noah

Ham   Shem   Japheth

b Find the seven missing links, using Genesis 11:10–25.

Terah

Abram = Sarai   Nahor = Milcah   Haran

Ishmael   **Isaac**   Lot

Jacob   Esau

Did you know ABRAM and ABRAHAM are the same person!

c Find out about two of the highlighted people using a Bible dictionary.

2 Now find out about your own family tree. Does your family tree influence which religion you follow?

STANDING UP FOR THE TRUTH

3 Who speaks out now?

Collect some newspaper cuttings about people or organizations which say that there are some things wrong with the way we live now.

You could organize them into different types, e.g.
a) violence
b) animal rights
c) nuclear war.

4 Some of the people who fight for things like animal rights sometimes break the law and get arrested.

a Do you think that people who believe that something is wrong should go as far as breaking the law?

b What do you feel strongly about, and what can you do about it?

Some suggestions to help you organize your thoughts:

A   Write a letter to a newspaper or your MP.
B   Ring a 'phone-in line to express your views.
C   Organize a petition.

Now:

5 a Design and conduct a survey in your class to see what your friends feel strongly about. (Look at the outline of a survey that has been drawn up for you, and use this to help you decide how your survey form should look.)

b In your books, write down what you discovered from your survey.

c Write down your list of suggestions for actually doing something about one of these problems.

6 a Copy and complete the following chart by looking up the Bible references in Column A. Write the name of the prophet who spoke out against the King in Column B. Write down what the King had done wrong in Column C.

b Discuss the reasons why you think people are prepared to stand up for what they believe is right.

A Bible reference	B Prophet	C What the King had done wrong
2 Samuel 12:1–7		
1 Kings 21:17–21		

7 What do you feel strongly about?

Survey form

Name: Martin Williams

AGE: (tick the correct box)

Under 11 ☐
11–13 ☑
14–16 ☐

a Which of the following makes you angry? (Tick as appropriate)

(i) Treating animals badly. ✓

(ii) Performing tests for cosmetics on animals. ✓

(iii) Medical research using animals.

(iv) Vandalised telephone boxes.

(v) American nuclear weapons in Britain.

(vi) People protesting against nuclear weapons.

(vii) Police brutality. ✓

(viii) Others (please list).
People being unfair.

b Would you join a demonstration for any of the following? (Tick as appropriate)

(i) More pay for nurses.

(ii) Abolition of aerosol cans which break down the ozone layer. ✓

(iii) Abolition of cosmetic tests on animals. ✓

(iv) A political party.

(v) Shortening the school holidays.

(vi) Others (please list).

HOW PEOPLE RECORD THEIR HISTORY

8 Think hard

a Why is the Old Testament included on this box?

b What is different about the Old Testament's way of recording history?

c Why do you think Israel's history was important to Jews?

9 Discuss

You might like to discuss these questions in small groups first. Then, after you have collected some ideas, report your ideas to the whole class.

a Do you think God is still involved in everyday events?

b How is he involved?

c Should this make a difference to the way we record our history?

THE OLD TESTAMENT

2000 YEARS OF JEWISH HISTORY IN ONE VOLUME

A Greenpeace ship

''The Lord said to Abraham, leave your country, your people, and your father's household, and go to the land I will show you . . . so Abraham left, as the Lord had told him.''
(Genesis 12:1)

Jews believe that the land of Israel is the land which God promised to Abraham. God also promised that Abraham's descendants would be a great nation:

''I will make you into a great nation, and I will bless you.''
(Genesis 12:2)

Both Jews and **Muslims** believe that they are Abraham's descendants. Jews believe that they are descended from Abraham through his son Isaac who was born when Abraham and Sarah were very old. Look in Genesis 21 for the story of Isaac's birth.

Muslims believe that they are also descended from Abraham, but through his eldest son Ishmael. You can find the story of Ishmael's birth in Genesis 16.

Both Jews and Muslims think that the promise of the land refers to themselves. This is part of the reason for the differences of opinion between Jews and Palestinians in Israel in the late twentieth century.

Later on, Abraham's descendants had to go to Egypt because there was a famine in the land of Israel. They were there for several hundred years. At first they were liked, and soon they began to have many children. The Egyptians started to get worried because they thought there would soon be more Hebrews than there were Egyptians. They forced the Hebrews (or people of Israel) to be slaves. They kept on making them work harder and harder, until the people of Israel wanted to leave Egypt and to return to their own land. A great leader called Moses helped them. After many adventures (which you can read about in **Exodus**), the people of Israel managed to leave Egypt.

For a long time they wandered around in the desert between Egypt and Israel. During this time they were given the Torah, including the **Ten Commandments**. These were to help them to live the kind of lives God wanted them to live. Jews, Christians and many other people use the Ten Commandments as the basis of their laws.

After forty years of wandering, the people of Israel arrived in the Promised Land. They crossed the River Jordan at a place called Jericho, near to the Dead Sea. They had to fight against the local inhabitants. It took a long time for them to be able to settle down in Israel (or **Canaan** as it was called then). The local inhabitants were very strong, and went on fighting for the land. Eventually the people of Israel were more powerful, and the other nations were defeated.

They always believed that it was God himself who led them out of Egypt and who gave them the land of Israel to live in. The prophets, who told the people what God wanted them to do, warned them not to forget about God when they settled down and started getting rich (Deuteronomy 8:11).

The time when the people of Israel left Egypt is called the Exodus. This is how Jews now remember the Exodus:

''My father was a wandering Aramean. He went down into Egypt with a few people and lived there. They became a large, powerful nation. But the Egyptians ill-treated us, and made us suffer. They forced us to be slaves. Then we cried out to the Lord, the God of our Fathers, and the Lord heard our voice. He saw our misery and how badly we were being treated. So the Lord brought us out of Egypt, using many miracles, and brought us into this land.''
(Deuteronomy 26:5–9)

NOTES/DATABASE

Use the glossary to look up the meanings of the following words. Then use the definitions to make your own notes or suitable entries on your database.

Jews	Ten Commandments
Muslims	Canaan
Exodus	

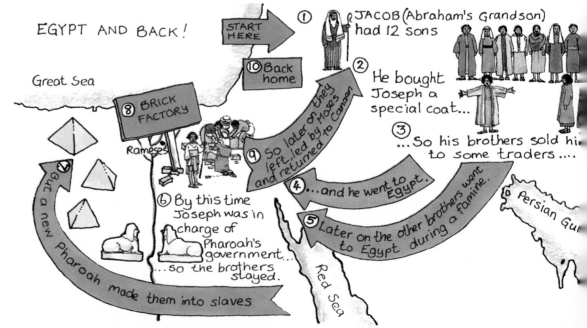

EGYPT AND BACK!

ACTIVITIES

1 Quick quiz

a Why do Jews believe that they are descended from Abraham?

b Why do Muslims believe that they are descended from Abraham?

c What were the promises which God made to Abraham?

d Why did Abraham's descendants have to go to Egypt?

e Why did the Egyptians begin to get worried?

f What did the Egyptians make the Israelites do?

g What was the name of the great leader who helped the people of Israel return to the Promised Land?

h Why were they given the Ten Commandments?

i Why did it take a long time for them to settle down properly in the Promised Land?

j Who did the people believe really led them out of Egypt and into the Promised Land?

k What did the prophets warn them about?

FLOOD WARNING!

"Here is the weather forecast for the next 48 hours. The weather will be warm and sunny. There will be a warm breeze. It is not expected to rain. Throughout the region the weather will remain stable!"

The Jews were not the only people in the ancient Near East who told the story of a great flood which covered the whole of the area they knew about. It is also in the *Epic of Gilgamesh*, a story found by archaeologists. Gilgamesh was told to build a boat. It was made of wood and covered with pitch. It was a huge construction, six floors high. It took thirty thousand barrels of pitch to cover the wood to make it waterproof.

This is what Gilgamesh says:

"All my silver and gold was loaded aboard her. All the animals I had were loaded too. I made all my family and relations get aboard, as well as all the craftsmen. There were wild animals as well as domestic ones . . .

"I looked at the weather, it was frightening, so I entered my vessel and closed the door . . . For seven days the wind blew and flood and storm swept the land. On the seventh day, the rain stopped and the storm and flood subsided . . . I looked at the sea. There was silence, the whole of mankind had turned to clay. When I looked out again, mountain ranges had appeared . . . and the vessel had got stuck on Mount Nsair . . .

"Seven days after arriving, I freed a dove, but it returned . . . then I freed a swallow, but that couldn't find a resting place either . . . then a raven . . . which did not return."

So finally, Gilgamesh prepared an offering to the gods. The gods promised that he would be like them and never die.

2 a Read both versions of the story of the flood.

b Copy and complete the chart below.

Questions	Genesis	Epic of Gilgamesh
a Who is the main character?		
b How was the boat built?		
c Who went in the boat?		
d Which animals went?		
e How long did the flood last?		
f Where did the boat land?		
g Which birds were sent out?		
h What promise did God make after the boat landed?		

3 Discuss

Read Genesis 9:8 – 17. Do you think God will keep his promise?

FURTHER ACTIVITIES

DAILY UR 1900 BCE

ABRAHAM HEARS GOD'S VOICE

Abraham and his wife Sarah have been popular figures in Ur for more than fifty years. Their marriage was one of the biggest social events this city has ever known. Now, however, it would seem that Abraham is beginning to go crazy! Recently, he has often been absent from the Ziggurat. Moon worship has not seemed complete since Abraham stopped attending. It is rumoured that the child sacrifices have been upsetting both Abraham and Sarah. They can't have any children themselves, though.

Sarah was recently heard to say that she thought it was a waste of human life to sacrifice a child to the moon god. She would rather offend the gods. She does not seem to realize what a privilege it is to have your child chosen to be sacrificed to the moon god!

Abraham has apparently been hearing voices. He claims that

A Ziggurat

these are the voice of God. When asked which god, he said, "The One God, who created the world." It seems this god told him that he was to leave Ur, and go camping! Abraham is intending to take his family and all his cattle, and to go to live in a tent! When asked where, Abraham said, "Wherever God tells me." God has, so Abraham says, promised to give Abraham a land of his own. He has also promised that Abraham's children will be a great nation. Abraham hasn't shown any signs of producing children yet! Is the voice of a new god going to make a difference?

1 Read the newspaper report.

Now read Genesis 12:1–5. What do you think happened?

Write a letter to the Editor of the Daily Ur explaining what you think. Use

Genesis 12:1–5 to help you work out why you think Abraham was prepared to leave his own land and go wherever God told him to.

2 Some people today are prepared to listen to the voice of God and to leave their homes to go where he wants to send them.

Some of these people are missionaries. You might like to write to a Missionary Society to ask them to send you some information about

missionaries and the way God leads and guides them today.

Here is an address which might be useful:

The Church Missionary Society,
156 Waterloo Road,
LONDON
SE1

ON THE MOVE!

3 The Sons of Jacob went to Egypt to look for food when there was a famine in their own country.

Look at this map of Egypt.

a What is the name of the river?

b What do you think that the land near the river might be like?

c Why do you think the Israelites knew that there was likely to be food in Egypt?

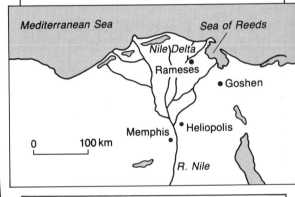

4 Find out more about Eygpt

a What kind of crops grow in Egypt?

b See what you can find out about Egypt's history.

c Find out what the following words mean:

Pharoah   pyramid

B River Nile, Luxor

5 Looking for food

a Why do people leave their homes in search of food?

b Try to collect some pictures of places in the world where there has been a famine recently. You may find some pictures of camps where people are given food. Some people have travelled hundreds of miles to the food stations. Many people have died on the way.

c Find out how Christian Aid and other charities have tried to help people in the Third World who have no food.

The address of Christian Aid is: PO Box 100, LONDON SE1 7RT.

6 Read Exodus 1:1–14.

a Why was the new king worried by the Israelites?

b What did the Egyptians do to the Israelites?

c What kind of jobs were they given?

d If you had been one of the Egyptians, would you have thought it was a good idea to make the Israelites slaves? Write down some reasons for your answer.

e If you had been one of the Israelites, how would you have felt about being forced to be a slave?

LIVING IN HARMONY

7 Group work

You have arrived on a new planet. It is very similar to Earth. If everyone works hard, you will be able to grow enough food. You have some domesticated farm animals. There is plenty of water, and you have brought enough seed for next year's crops.

Make a list of the basic rules which you will need to help you all to **live happily** together on this new planet.

8 Now read Exodus 20, where you will find the Ten Commandments.

Copy and complete the chart.

There is a modern version of each Commandment in Column A. Use the Bible version to match the correct Commandment from Exodus to the modern version. Enter this in Column B. In Column C put the rule which you thought of for your new planet which matches the Bible Commandment most closely. Don't worry if you have some gaps in Column C.

Add to Column C any extra rules which you have thought of.

Hundreds of years after they first had the Ten Commandments, the Israelites boasted that their God was best because he gave them the most sensible rules to help them to know how to behave. Other nations' gods demanded child sacrifice as well as other horrific things. Israel's religion was always full of sound common sense.

A Modern version	B Bible	C New planet rule
1 Worship God.		
2 Don't worship material things (manufactured things).		
3 Don't misuse the name of God.		
4 Have a real day off once a week – for everyone, including the animals.		
5 Look after old people.		
6 Don't murder.		
7 Don't make love to anyone who is married to someone else.		
8 Don't steal.		
9 Don't tell lies which get other people into trouble.		
10 Don't start wanting things which belong to other people.		

9 Discuss

Do you agree that most rules are a matter of common sense? Give your reasons.

We have already found out that the Old Testament is important for three different religions: **Judaism**, **Christianity**, and **Islam**. Each of these religions believe in one God. They are called **monotheistic** religions. They are also **revealed** religions. This means that they teach about a God who wants to make himself known to people. The God of the Old Testament is one who is looking for people. The first question in the Old Testament is, "Adam, where are you?". This is the keynote of the Old Testament. It teaches about a God who reveals himelf to ordinary people.

Throughout the Old Testament God guides his people. Sometimes, when they don't do as he tells them, he gets angry with them. There are times when he is

A "God saw what he had made, and it was all good." (Genesis 1:3)

pleased with them, and times when he punishes them. There is never a time when he is not there. He is interested in everything they do, and listens when they want to talk to him. He looks after them in good times and in bad times. He is absolutely reliable and is always with them.

The God of the Old Testament is a personal God. He is real to individuals who put their trust in him. He is also a person who has real feelings of love, anger and every other emotion.

If you want to know what this God is like, then the Old Testament says you should look at the best of what is in people. Genesis 1:26 says that when God made people in the first place, he made them 'in his own image'. In other words, people are like God.

Judaism, Christianity and Islam never argue for the existence of God. The Old Testament treats the existence of God as an obvious fact. It teaches that God is the Creator of the Universe.

There are two stories of Creation in Genesis. In each story, God is the Creator. He made everything. The order in which he made things differs in each story. The fact that he made everything is treated as undeniable truth in each story (Genesis 1:1 – 2:3, and Genesis 2:4 – 24).

Much of the Old Testament is history. Judaism and Christianity are both built firmly on what God has done for his people in history. The Exodus, when the people of Israel left Egypt, was something which happened in history. It is something which God did. It was God who led the Israelites out of Egypt. He used Moses, but without God it would never have happened (Deuteronomy 26:8).

In some ways the Old Testament has a very straightforward view of life. If people do what God wants, then things will go well for them. If they are disobedient, then things will not go well. It's very simple. Look at what Moses says to the

people of Israel in Deuteronomy 30:1 – 10. The people are offered a choice. Obey God, and he will continue to look after them. They are commanded to love God, and then they will be prosperous. But the warning is that if they wander away from God, they will be destroyed.

B "God created human beings." (Genesis 1:27)

The God of the Old Testament is one who loves his people. In return for the way in which he looks after them, he expects them to love him and to be obedient to him.

> Isaiah 43:1b-2a
>
> "Do not be afraid –
> I will save you.
> I have called you by name –
> you are mine.
> When you pass through deep waters,
> I will be with you;
> your troubles will not overwhelm you."

NOTES/DATABASE

Use the glossary to look up the meanings of the following words. Then use the definitions to make your own notes or suitable entries on your database.

Judaism	Monotheistic
Islam	Revealed

KEY IDEAS ABOUT GOD IN THE OLD TESTAMENT

a There is one God.
b God reveals himself to ordinary people.
c God guides his people.
d God is always present with his people.
e God is personal.
f God is both loving and just.
g God created the world.
h God created people to be like himself.
i God acts in history.
j God can always be trusted.

ACTIVITIES

GOD GUIDES HIS PEOPLE

Exodus 13:17 – Across the desert

God used  and

in the daytime

at night to help his people across the desert.

Later on people always expected God to be with them when they saw clouds or fire. This was why there was fire on the day of Pentecost in Acts 2.

It helped the disciples to understand that God was really with them.

> The best way to find out what God is like is to find out what he does!

1 Copy the map of the route the Israelites took from Egypt to the Promised Land.

You might like to make a game using the map and the route they took. Use the questions from the quick quizzes in other chapters to help with your game.

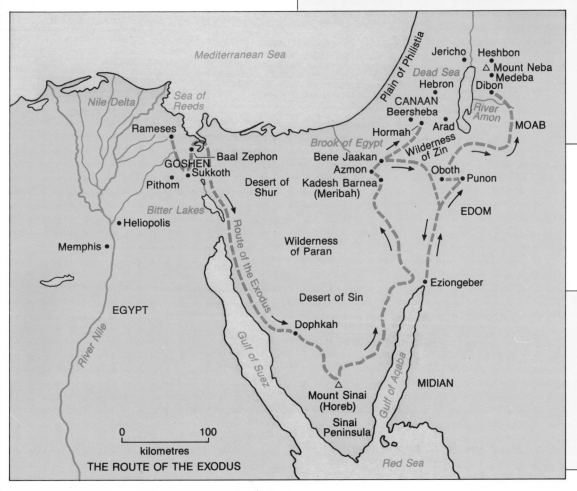

THE ROUTE OF THE EXODUS

FURTHER ACTIVITIES

1 In the Bible people often needed special signs to show them that God was with them.

Copy the chart below. Look up the references in Column A, then complete Columns B and C.

A Reference	B Person	C Sign
Exodus 3:2		
Isaiah 6:6f		
I Kings 19:12f		
Mark 1:10f		
Mark 9:7f		
Acts 2:4		

Christians today have a sign of God's presence. When they receive the bread and wine at Communion, this is a sign to each of them that Jesus is really with them.

C The Eucharist

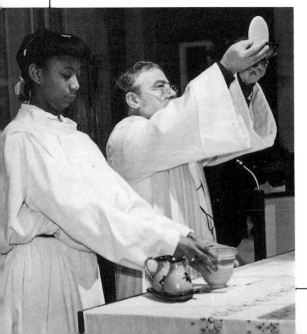

2 **Discuss**

What would the perfect person be like?

Make a list of qualities you think he/she would have.

3 Here is a list of some of the things which the Old Testament says about God.

Tick off the qualities of the perfect person from your list which match the qualities of God.

Now tick off the qualities you have.

Qualities of God	Qualities of the perfect person	MY qualities
a good		
b kind		
c slow to anger		
d reliable		
e always there when you want him		
f leads and guides		
g loving		
h faithful		
i cares about everyone		
j considerate towards others		
k absolutely fair		

4 **Discuss**
Is there anything you would like to add to this list of qualities of God?

Remember

a Jesus, who Christians believe was the Son of God, was the perfect person.

b Christians, Jews and Muslims all believe that people are made in the image of God.

SOME WAYS IN WHICH THE OLD TESTAMENT DESCRIBES GOD

5 Look up Psalm 23 in your Bible.

a How is God (the Lord) described in this Psalm?

b What are God's people likened to in this Psalm?

c Make a list of things which the Psalmist (the person who wrote the Psalm) says that God does for him.

d How does God help when the writer is afraid?

e How does the writer show that he is sure that God is always with him?

6 Copy and complete the chart below.

In the first column make a list of the things which you would expect a shepherd to do for his sheep.

In the second column make a list of the things which you have discovered so far that Israelites believes God does for them.

Some of the items in each list may be the same. If so, write them on your chart next to each other.

You may need to add to the second column later.

Things a shepherd does for his sheep	Things God does for his people

7 a Look up the following references.

(i) Psalm 24:7
(ii) Psalm 44:4
(iii) Psalm 47:7

b What word is used to describe God in each reference?

c How do you think it adds to the Old Testament picture of God when he is described as 'King'?

d Look up the following references, and write down the word which is used to describe God.

(i) Psalm 7:8
(ii) Psalm 9:8
(iii) Psalm 50:6

e How do you think it adds to the Old Testament idea of God to think of him as a judge?

8 **Discuss**

How can God be described as both loving and a judge?

Is it possible to be both?

9 King David, who wrote Psalm 23, was a shepherd when he was a young boy.

He knew all about looking after sheep, and what to do to look after them properly. He also wrote the other Psalms you have been asked to look at.

a Why do you think that King David chose to describe God as:
(i) shepherd
(ii) King
(iii) Judge?

b Now it's your turn to write a Psalm. How are you going to describe God? David used things he knew about. How would it be meaningful for you to think about God? You might like to draw a picture which fits in with your Psalm.

AGREEMENTS

or Bargains
or Covenants

God's agreement with Israel.
"If you obey me and keep my commandments then I will be your God and you will be my people."
(Jeremiah 11:4)

I accept the place at Fulston Manor School and agree to keep the rules.
Signed .....*Richard Isaac*...........

10 a What agreements have you made this week?

b Copy the chart below and list them in the first column. List any other kinds of agreements. Then say who the people involved are in the next two columns. Two examples are entered for you.

What happened	Person 1	Person 2
a bought pop star magazine	me	newsagent
b cleaning the car	my sister	dad

11 God had a special agreement with Israel.

It was called a covenant. Look at 2 Chronicles 7:15.

Now answer these questions.

a Who were the two people (or groups of people) involved in this agreement?

b What did Israel have to do?

c What did God promise if Israel kept its side of the bargain?

d What do you think God might want his people to do now, as part of an agreement with them?

e What do you think God would promise now as his side of the bargain?

f Write the covenant between God and Israel as if it was you and God who were involved.

WHAT IT TELLS US ABOUT PEOPLE

The Old Testament is almost like a play with two main characters: God and people. Each of the Creation stories in Genesis tells us about the Creation of people. In each story people are clearly the most important part of Creation.

We have only one earth...

and there are five billion of us

sharing it.

POVERTY & HOPE · POVERTY & HOPE · POVERTY & HOPE · POVERTY & HOPE · POVERTY & HOPE

The Hebrew word for man is **Adam**. This is why, in English, the name of the first man is Adam. The Hebrew Bible simply says 'man' every time you read the name 'Adam'. The stuff from which Adam was made is called, in Hebrew, 'Adamah'. We usually translate this as 'dust' or 'soil'. It helps to remember that Adam is made from Adamah . . . or stuff for making Adams with!

In each story, the woman is very important. She was created as an equal partner with man. In Genesis 1:27, man and woman were created at the same time. The other story, in Genesis 2:22, says that woman was created as a helper or partner for the man, and was actually made out of the man's own body. In each case, they are clearly meant to be partners in the work which God has planned for them to do. Their job is to look after the Earth. They have to look after the animals and the crops.

In each of the stories in Genesis, the man and the woman were intended to be in charge of the Earth. God would always be there to help them, but the task of looking after all the plants and animals in the world belonged to them.

People were created to be special. In Genesis 1, the creation of people was the most important part of Creation. People were made last. When everything was ready for them, people were created to take their proper place in charge of everything on Earth.

In the other story, in Genesis 2, people were made before all the animals. As they were created, the different animals were given into the care of Adam and Eve. People were created to take responsibility for the world.

People were created to be like God. That doesn't mean they would have the same kind of power and authority as God. However, they received power and authority from God to do the job of looking after the world. Genesis 1:26 makes it very clear that people are copies of God. "Let us make man in our own image," he says. That means that we can know something of what God is like, by knowing what the very best qualities are in people.

The Old Testament picture is that people were created to rule the world. However, the Old Testament is not blind to the fact that human nature is not always good, noble and unselfish. It recognizes that people can also have bad

A People in control

B Keeping in touch

motives, and choose to do wrong things. The story of Adam and Eve being thrown out of the Garden of Eden for disobedience is an attempt to explain how evil came into the world.

Throughout the Old Testament, first of all Adam and Eve and then Israel, are seen as having to make a choice between good and evil. What God wants his people to do is always good, but they sometimes (often) choose evil.

The fact that people often choose to do what they know to be wrong is called 'sin'. In the Bible, sin is the same as being disobedient to what people know God wants them to do. Put another way, it is going their own way, despite many warnings that they should go God's way. Even though people choose to disobey God in the Old Testament, God never gives up on them. He always goes on loving and caring. Eventually, he promises to write his Law in peoples' hearts, so that they won't need anyone to tell them that they're doing wrong (Jeremiah 31:31–33).

Finally, the Old Testament promise is that God will send a very special person who will lead and guide people and help them to live the way God wants them to. The Jews are still waiting for this special person, called the Messiah. Christians believe that Jesus of Nazareth was the Messiah.

ACTIVITIES

1 Quick quiz

a Which is the most important part of Creation?

b Explain why the name for the first man is 'Adam' in English.

c What was Adam made from?

d What was the main job of the first man and woman?

e What does Genesis 1:26 say about people?

f Which Old Testament story tries to explain why some people do wrong?

g What do you think 'sin' means?

h How does God promise to help his people do what he wants them to do?

i Who are some Jews waiting for?

j Who do Christians believe the special person sent by God is?

2 Who does the new baby take after?

We've all got pictures of ourselves as children.

Try to find an old picture of yourself when you were little. Do you look like any of your relations?

Have you inherited any of their skills?

C Copying Dad

3 Discuss

a Do your parents ever say, "You are just like your mother/father."? Try and make a list of any family characteristics you may have. Sometimes children copy the way they behave from people they spend a lot of time with. Did you?

b Do you think that people have any of the same qualities as God? What makes God different from people?

4 a Look up Genesis 1:26. What does this tell us about what God intended (according to the Old Testament) when he made people?

b Have you ever heard anyone say, "She is the image of her mother/aunt"? What do you think they mean when they say this?

c Read Psalm 8. This is all about God and his relationship with people.
 (i) Which verse says that God cares about people?
 (ii) Which verse says that people are important?
 (iii) Which verse says that God has given people the job of looking after all the things on Earth?

FURTHER ACTIVITIES

PARTNERS

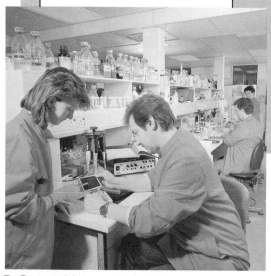

D Partnership

1 Proverbs 31 is often called the pattern for the perfect woman.

Read carefully Proverbs 31:10–31.

Now copy and complete the following chart. In Column A put all the things which the perfect woman does in the Bible reading. In Column B put all the things which you think a woman ought to do. If some of them are the same, place them next to each other. You may have some extra ones in each column.

Column A	Column B

2 **Discuss**

a In the stories in Genesis, do you think the man or the woman was the more important?

b (i) Do you think men and women should always be allowed to do the same jobs?
(ii) Are there any jobs which you think should be done only by men?
(iii) Are there any jobs which you think should be done only by women?

Now:

Write down some reasons for the answers you have given.

E Working can be fun

GOD'S PROMISES APPLY TO EVERYBODY!

The Old Testament sees men and women together as partners in the great adventure of looking after God's world. They sometimes have different jobs to do, but neither man nor woman is more important. In God's eyes they are partners.

F Our daily bread

3 **Discuss**

What are your views? Do you think men and women have the same part to play in the world? Do you think they are different but equally important? Or perhaps you think that one is more important than the other?

4 Something to think about

When you have refused to do as you are told at school, how do you feel:
a at the time,
b later?

If you have been punished for refusing to do as you are told, or for breaking a rule which everyone knows about, how do you react?

Are you angry?

Do you say, "It's not fair"?

Do you sometimes think you might deserve to be punished?

WOMAN THROWN OUT FOR REFUSING TO PAY RENT

Man Imprisoned for Refusal to Obey Court Order

GIRL THROWN OUT OF DISCO!

GARDEN OF EDEN rules

DO NOT EAT FRUIT FROM THE TREE IN THE MIDDLE.

Owner-God

5 Look carefully at the headlines on this page.

a Look at the headline about the disco. What kind of thing do you think might have happened?

b Write a short story about an incident at a disco in which someone got thrown out.

c In groups:

Select one of the other headlines on this page. Work out what the story behind the headline might have been. Now either act out the story for the rest of your class, or record a short play which explains what happened to create that headline.

Man and Woman Thrown out of Garden for Disobeying the Owner's Instructions

6 What kind of story is behind this headline?

G 'Look after the Earth'

WHY WORK?

7 Which of these statements do you agree with?
(You may select more than one.)

a) I don't see why I should work for a living.

b) I enjoy work.

c) I only enjoy myself when I'm not working.

d) I work so that I can eat.

e) A good balance of work and play is important.

8 Discuss

a Why do people need to work?

b What different kinds of work are there?

c Make a list of the various jobs you would like to do under these three headings:

(i) services to people
(ii) technical services
(iii) business and administration.

ATTITUDES TO WORK

Work is such a good idea only God could have thought of it.

By working, a person has control over their own life.

Situations vacant
EDEN NURSERIES
full time gardener – hours negotiable
grow your own food

Work is a privilege which is God-given.

When Adam and Eve were disobedient in the story of the Garden of Eden (Genesis), God sent them out to work. No longer would everything be provided for them. They must now take responsibility for their own lives by growing crops.

Later (Psalm 8), people are said to have authority over everything on Earth. Their job is to look after the day to day running of the world.

They are not expected simply to sit back and let God provide for them. They are supposed to learn responsibility for the world around them.

9 Discuss

As you have grown up, how have you begun to take more responsibility
a at home b at school?

For a very long time, **Jews** have been expecting a special person. This person is called the **Messiah**. The name 'Messiah' means 'the **anointed** one'. He is expected to be sent by God. Part of his job will be to lead and guide God's people.

The Jews are still waiting for this Messiah to come. Christians believe that Jesus of Nazareth was this special person.

How did the Jews know that God was going to send the Messiah?

Several hundred years before Jesus was born, the **prophets** began to explain to the rest of the people that God was going to send a special messenger. Prophets are people who explain the Word of God to everyone else. They always explained God's messages in ways which everyone could understand.

A Jews believe that when the Messiah comes he will enter Jerusalem through the Golden Gate

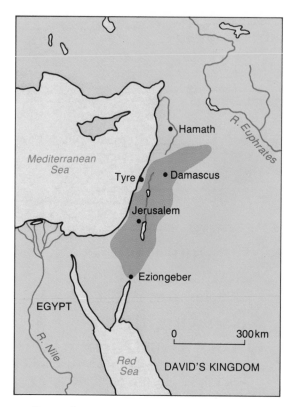

DAVID'S KINGDOM

B David was a shepherd before he became King

One of the most famous kings that Israel had was King David. He had been a shepherd when he was a young boy. His family had lived in the little hill town of Bethlehem. His father was called Jesse. The family kept sheep. Bethlehem was called the 'town of David' because David's family lived there.

King David was very much loved by all his people. When he was king, Israel won many great victories over other nations. Later on, the prophets began to say that there was going to be a new leader, who would be like David and would be from David's family.

This is what Isaiah says:

"For to us a child is born
to us a son is given,
and the government will be upon his shoulders.
And he will be called
Wonderful Counsellor,
Mighty God,
Everlasting Father,
The Prince of Peace.

Of the increase of his government and peace there will be no end.
He will reign on David's throne and over his kingdom.''
(Isaiah 9:6–7)

At roughly the same time another prophet called Micah even knew the name of the town where the Messiah would be born. This is what he says:

"But you Bethlehem . . . out of you will come forth the one who will be the ruler over Israel.''
(Micah 5:2)

This is the section of the Bible which King Herod's wise men looked at to find out where the wise men should go to find the baby who was to be called 'King of the Jews'. You can find this part of the story of Jesus in Matthew 2:3–4.

The Old Testament says a great deal about the birth of Jesus. It also says what his job was going to be.

In the time of Jesus the Jews had two main ideas about the Messiah and what he would be like:

1 Some of them expected a strong military leader like David. They wanted someone who would drive out the Romans and make Israel into a great nation again.

2   Others expected a man who would know about the lives of ordinary people. They expected him to help them in many ways. These words from Isaiah are what many Jews expected the Messiah to say:

"The Spirit of the Lord is upon me because the Lord has anointed me to preach the good news to the poor. He has sent me to bind up the broken hearted . . . and to proclaim the year of the Lord's favour."
(Isaiah 61:1–2)

Read Luke 4:16–19 to discover what Jesus believed the Messiah's job was like.

NOTES/DATABASE

Use the glossary to look up the meanings of the following words. Then use the definitions to make your own notes or entries on your database.

Jew	Anointed
Messiah	Prophet

ACTIVITIES

1 a Someone special

The Jews expected someone special called a Messiah (the Greek word is Christos, or Christ) to come and live with them and be their king.

Look up the following Bible references which Christians believe refer to the Messiah.

Isaiah 7:14   Isaiah 9:6–8
Micah 5:2

Now use the information in these verses to answer these questions about the Messiah.

a   Was his mother going to be young or old?

b   What was the Messiah's name going to be?

c   What does this name mean?

d   Which King is he going to be descended from?

e   What special names will the Messiah be given?

f   Which town is he going to be born in?

Now look up these New Testament references and answer the same questions about the Messiah.

Matthew 1:23, 2:5
Luke 1:26–33

2 Discuss

Do you know anyone who has recently had a new baby?

What kind of things do people do to get ready for a new baby?

In your groups, make a list of the different ways that people prepare themselves for the birth of a baby.

Now:

Discuss what kind of things God did to prepare people for the birth of the Messiah.

C The new baby

Why do you think the prophets knew so much about him so long before he was born?

3 Getting ready for the new baby

God used the prophets Isaiah and Micah to tell people that there was going to be a very special baby.

Use the lists you made in your discussion to help you to compare the way in which people today prepare for the birth of a baby and the way God prepared the family of Israel for the birth of a very special baby. Copy and complete the chart.

Question	People now	God
a When were people told there was a baby on the way?		
b Who was the first to know?		
c Who was told next?		
d How did they find out that they were going to have a baby?		

THE MESSIAH IN THE OLD TESTAMENT

FURTHER ACTIVITIES

PREPARE THE WAY OF THE LORD

Try to listen to the record or tape of the song 'Prepare ye the way of the Lord' from *Godspell* by Stephen Schwartz.

In the Old Testament God promised to send someone to 'prepare the way of the Lord'.

1 Look up Isaiah 40:3 and 9–10, and Malachi 4:5.

a Where was the person going to be who was 'preparing the way'?

b How was he going to prepare?

c Who was going to come again before the 'Day of the Lord'?

d Which towns would the people come from who would hear the good news?

e What would the person say (Isaiah 40:9–10)?

D Prepare the way of the Lord

2 Now read Mark 1:1–8.

a Why do you think John the Baptist came just before Jesus?

b What did John the Baptist think his job was?

c Why do you think some people thought he might be Elijah or the Messiah?

3 Using all the Bible references on this page, complete a chart like the one below.

Question	Old Testament	John
a When was the way to be prepared?		
b What did the messenger have to do?		
c Where did the people come from who heard about it?		

4 The Old Testament says that the messenger would say "Behold your God."

Use John 1:29. What did John the Baptist say about Jesus?

The Old Testament tells us a lot about what the Messiah was going to do.

Jesus said several times that he had come "as a servant". Once he even showed his disciples what he meant

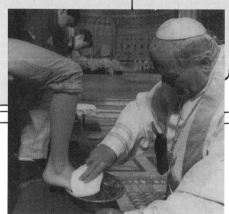

F Is this really what Jesus meant?

by wrapping a towel round himself and washing everyone's feet.

Do you think people were surprised when Jesus acted like this?

E Serving others

5 Read Isaiah 61:1–3

The person who is saying this is called the 'servant'.

Now look up Luke 4:16–20 and Luke 7:18–23.

a In what ways do you think Jesus thought he was like the 'servant' in Isaiah?

b What kind of things would you expect a servant to do?

6 Mother Teresa says that it is her job to work amongst the 'poorest of the poor' and to serve them.

Find out as much as you can about Mother Teresa and her work in Calcutta and all over the world. Do you think she thinks of herself as a 'servant'?

G A Sister of Mercy working in Calcutta

7 **Discuss**

How similar do you think Mother Teresa's way of being a servant is to Jesus' way?

"Rejoice greatly, O Daughter of Jerusalem. See, your King comes to you, . . . riding on a donkey." (Zechariah 3:9)

8 Look at Mark 11 to see how Jesus fulfilled this prophecy.

Make a list of the similarities you can find.

Jesus was eventually arrested, tried and executed. He suffered humiliation, torture and the most painful death possible. During his trial he said nothing in his own defence. He was beaten so that he became almost unrecognizable.

Christians believe that there was a reason for his death. They believe that on the cross, he received the punishment for sin that really belongs to human

H Jesus rode into Jerusalem on a donkey

beings. Because of that, if people really want to live their lives the way God wants them to, they may be forgiven for the evil they have done. The only condition is that they believe in Jesus. Finally, Jesus was buried in a borrowed grave which belonged to a rich man called Joseph of Arimathea. Three days later, Christians believe, Jesus came alive again.

Read Isaiah 53 very carefully. After Jesus had died, Christians started to believe that this referred to Jesus.

9 **Discuss**

What similarities can you see between what Isaiah 53 says and what actually happened to Jesus? Use John 18 and 19 to help you.

10 Jesus pointed to the story of Jonah (look at the story of Jonah again in Unit 1) as a sign that he would rise again from the dead.

Why do you think Jesus used this as a sign that he would rise again?

WHAT THE OLD TESTAMENT TELLS CHRISTIANS ABOUT JESUS

- He would be born in Bethlehem.
- He would be descended from King David.
- He was to be called Emmanuel, which means 'God is with us'. This means that people who met him would realize that they were meeting God.
- He would heal people.
- He would tell the poor people about God.
- He would be specially interested in the poor and the under-privileged.
- He would act like a servant, even though he was a king.
- He would care about people, and look after them.
- He would suffer.
- He would never do anything wrong.

In the Old Testament, the Spirit of God is always at work. In the second verse of the Bible, the 'Spirit of God' (Good News says the 'power of God') was moving over the surface of the water.

The Spirit of God is always linked with the power of God. The presence of God's spirit is accompanied by demonstrations of God's power. The Hebrew word for spirit is 'ruach'. It also means 'wind'. In Acts 2, when the **disciples** were given the gift of the Holy Spirit, there was a strong wind. This was one of the ways in which they knew that God was with them in a very powerful way.

Throughout the Old Testament God does things through the power of his spirit.

A "And God saw that everything He had made was very good indeed."

PROPHETS

Sometimes people are said to be filled with the Spirit. Moses and some of the **prophets** were described as having the Spirit of God. They were given the Spirit, or the power of God, for special reasons. For example, the craftsmen who worked on the tabernacle (the special place where the Israelites worshipped God in the desert) were given the Spirit of God to help them in their work.

Elisha was said to have the Spirit of God, which he inherited from Elijah. Find this story in 2 Kings 1–2.

KING SAUL

King Saul received God's Spirit to help him to be a good king. Later on, he became aware that the Spirit of God was no longer with him, but was with David instead.

The Holy Spirit was always given to people for good reasons. It was not just to make them feel good, or to make them think they were better than other people. It was so that they could do the work which God planned for them to do.

"God used the power of His Spirit to create the world."

"And God saw that everything he had made was very good indeed."

The prophets said that when the **Messiah** came, people would no longer need the **Law**, which had been written on stone tablets. Instead, they would have God's Law written in their hearts and minds (Jeremiah 31:31–33). The way this was to happen was through the gift of the Holy Spirit.

B "Your old men will dream dreams."

JOEL

The prophet Joel lived in troubled times. He told of a great disaster, and the need for everyone to pray. If everyone prayed, Joel said, God would spare people.

"This is what God says", Joel declared. "I will repay the years that the locusts have eaten." What do you think God meant by this?

Then Joel went on to say that God promised to give the gift of the Holy Spirit to everyone:

"Afterwards I will pour out my Spirit on everyone;
Your sons and daughters will proclaim my message;
Your old men will have dreams,
and your young men will see visions.
At that time I will pour out my spirit even on servants, both men and women."

THE SPIRIT IS FOR EVERYONE

This is the first time that the Holy Spirit has been promised to everyone. Before this, in the Old Testament, it has been given to prophets and kings. These were people who had special work to do for God. In the book of Joel it is promised to everyone, whatever their status, even servants. The Old Testament recognized

C Procession of Bishops, Lambeth Conference 1988

that God wanted everyone to do his work, and so his Holy Spirit was to be given to everyone who was prepared to serve him. The promise of the Spirit is the final piece in the Old Testament jigsaw. The stage is now set for the entry of the Messiah.

NOTES/DATABASE

Use the glossary to look up the meanings of the following words. Then use the definitions to make your own notes or suitable entries for your database.

Disciple   Messiah

Prophet   Law

ACTIVITIES

GIDEON FIGHTS A BATTLE

1 Gideon was said to have the Spirit of God. He was given it to be able to lead Israel in battle.

Read Judges 6:34–40.

How did Gideon make sure God was with him? Use Judges 6:33–40 to draw a series of pictures – these could be made to look like a film strip – about the way in which Gideon proved (twice) that God was with him. Other judges (leaders were called judges before they had kings) also received the Spirit of God.

Look up these references. Copy and complete with the name of the person opposite the reference.

Reference	Person
Judges 11:29	
Judges 13:25	

2 **Quick quiz**

a What is the first time that the Spirit of God is mentioned in the Bible?

b What is the Spirit of God always linked with?

c What is the Hebrew word for spirit?

D The place where Gideon fought his battle

d Make a list of some of the people in the Old Testament who are said to be filled with the Spirit of God.

e Why did the craftsmen receive the Spirit?

f From whom did Elisha inherit the Spirit?

g Why did the kings of Israel need the gift of the Spirit?

h How were the people helped to do the work God planned for them?

i Where was the new Law going to be carved?

j Who, according to Joel, would receive the Spirit of God?

k Before this, who were the only people to have the Spirit of God?

FURTHER ACTIVITIES

INSPIRATION: The Spirit at work

Do you need some 'inspiration' to help you paint a picture, make a model in pottery, or write a poem?

Did you know that the word 'inspire' also means 'to take in breath'?

We need 'inspiration' to help us create something. God is a bit different, though. He *breathed out* (or 'expired') when he created people and made them living beings (Genesis 2:7). This was the moment when people received their 'spirit' from God and this changed them into something special and different from the rest of creation.

So the spirit in people, according to the Bible, is very like God's Spirit because that's where people got it from in the first place.

However, there are some special times when, in the Old Testament, God gave people some extra 'inspiration' for special reasons. Here are a few individuals who needed it!

To build the tabernacle. — CRAFTSMEN

To govern Israel with Moses. — 70 ELDERS

To be a prophet. — ELISHA

To lead Israel out of Egypt and into the Promised Land. — MOSES

To be a prophet. — ELIJAH

To be a prophet, a leader of Israel and to choose who should be king. — SAMUEL

To be a great king. — DAVID

To be Israel's first king. — SAUL

1 Copy this diagram into your book.

Why do you think all these different people needed the 'inspiration' of the Spirit of God?

"I will breathe my spirit into them"

2 Read Ezekiel 37:1–14.

This story tells us about a vision that the prophet Ezekiel had. The vision explained that God is powerful enough to restore even dried-up bones to life.

a Draw a series of pictures which explain what you think happened in this story.

b What difference did God's Spirit (breath) make?

3 Look at the picture of the model of the Second Temple. It was rebuilt by Zerubbabel after it had been destroyed.

Look up Zechariah 4:6.

a How is Zerubbabel going to succeed?

b In what way do you think the Spirit of God could help in a task such as building a temple?

E Model of the second Temple

4 Look up Isaiah 61:1–3

The person speaking is the 'Servant of the Lord'.

Verses 1–3 contain a list of some of the things which the Servant, who is filled with God's Spirit, will do.

a What will the Servant do, now that he is filled with God's Spirit?

b Find out:
(i) In what ways are the things in this list done by Christians today?
(ii) How do you think they might be helped by the Spirit of God today?

F Forces chaplain at work

Tell these dry bones that God will bring them back to life!

Can these bones come back to life?

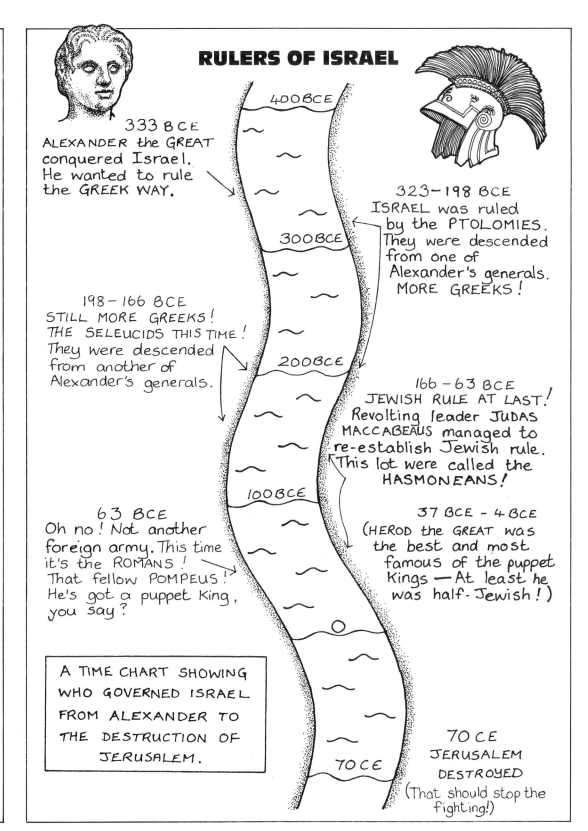

RULERS OF ISRAEL

400 BCE

333 BCE
ALEXANDER the GREAT conquered Israel. He wanted to rule the GREEK WAY.

323–198 BCE
ISRAEL was ruled by the PTOLOMIES. They were descended from one of Alexander's generals. MORE GREEKS!

300 BCE

198–166 BCE
STILL MORE GREEKS! THE SELEUCIDS THIS TIME! They were descended from another of Alexander's generals.

200 BCE

166–63 BCE
JEWISH RULE AT LAST! Revolting leader JUDAS MACCABEAUS managed to re-establish Jewish rule. This lot were called the HASMONEANS!

100 BCE

63 BCE
Oh no! Not another foreign army. This time it's the ROMANS! That fellow POMPEUS! He's got a puppet King, you say?

37 BCE – 4 BCE
(HEROD the GREAT was the best and most famous of the puppet Kings — At least he was half-Jewish!)

A TIME CHART SHOWING WHO GOVERNED ISRAEL FROM ALEXANDER TO THE DESTRUCTION OF JERUSALEM.

70 CE
JERUSALEM DESTROYED
(That should stop the fighting!)

70 CE

It is through the writers of the New Testament that we know about Jesus.

The first four books of the New Testament are known as **Gospels**. The word 'Gospel' means 'good news'. A Gospel, therefore, is a book which tells the 'good news' about Jesus. It includes details about the things which Jesus said as well as what he did.

Each of the four Gospels was written by a different person. They each tell the story from a slightly different point of view, just as different newspapers today give slightly different accounts of the same events. Some things which Jesus said or did are included in one Gospel but not in another, but the main events of Jesus' life are the same in each Gospel. Each of them seems to include some eye witness accounts of what happened.

Without Jesus, the New Testament would never have been written. He is the central character who dominates every page. Jesus changed people's lives. He lived for only thirty years in an obscure country of the Middle East, but he changed the world. He has had more influence on the world than anyone else in history. You don't have to be Christian to recognize the changes which have happened because people became followers of Jesus of Nazareth.

All four Gospels agree that Jesus was from Nazareth in Galilee. People began to notice him and follow him when he was about thirty years old. He was **baptized** in the River Jordan by John the Baptist. For about three years he went all over Israel preaching and teaching. Many people were healed by him. He was especially concerned that poor people should hear the 'good news' which he came to bring. This good news

B Luke 4:16f

was that anyone who believed in Jesus, and told God that they were sorry for the things which they had done wrong, could be part of God's Kingdom.

The religious authorities objected to some of Jesus' teaching. Eventually, Jesus was arrested and tried. The Romans sentenced him to death, and he was executed by **crucifixion**. Each of the New Testament writers agree that he was seen again alive three days later, and for the next forty days. This event is called the **Resurrection**. The whole of the Christian faith is built on the fact of the Resurrection. Paul says

''If Christ has not been raised from the dead, then your faith is worth nothing.'' (1 Corinthians 15:14)

There are twenty-seven books altogether in the New Testament. After the four Gospels comes the Acts of the Apostles. This is an exciting account of the early **Church** as it spread throughout the Roman Empire. It tells us a great deal about the lives of the first Christians. The adventures of Peter (one of Jesus' first disciples) and Paul (who started off by trying to kill Christians and then became one of them!) are told in some detail.

Peter and Paul each wrote letters to the Christians in the cities which they visited. These are included in the New

A Mark 1:1–12

Testament. There are many letters (or **Epistles**) in this section which answer questions about being a Christian. They give lots of good advice to try to help people to follow Jesus.

Finally, the Book of Revelation is a series of visions written by John, one of Jesus' disciples, when he was an old man. They were dangerous days for Christians, and some of it is written in a kind of code. It was safer that way, because from 64 CE onwards Christians were likely to be tortured and even put to death.

The New Testament was written to help and encourage Christians in difficult days as well as to teach them about Jesus. It has helped and encouraged people throughout history.

HELP!

Acts 20:7–12

Acts 9:23–25

Look up the Bible reference under each picture, and then write your own caption for each picture.

ACTIVITIES

1 Quick quiz

a Who is the central character of the New Testament?

b How can we find out about the life of Jesus of Nazareth?

c What are the first four books of the New Testament about?

d Why do the details of some of the stories about Jesus vary?

e What do all the Gospel writers agree about?

f Who, according to Jesus, could be part of God's Kingdom?

g Write down the names of two of the people who wrote letters which are included in the New Testament.

h Why was it necessary to write the Book of Revelation in a kind of code?

i What was one of the reasons for writing the New Testament?

8th Century BCE Birth of Jesus is announced.

4 BCE Birth of Jesus.

9 CE Jesus visited Jerusalem for his Bar Mitzvah.

27 CE Jesus was baptized in the River Jordan by John the baptist.

NOTES/DATABASE

Use the glossary to look up the meanings of the following words. Then use the definitions to make your own notes or suitable entries on your database.

Gospel	Resurrection
Baptize	Church
Crucifixion	Epistle

The ministry and teaching of Jesus.

30 CE The death and Resurrection of Jesus.

30 CE Gift of the Holy Spirit.

THE EARLY CHURCH

37 CE The conversion of St Paul.

PAUL OF TARSUS

ATHENS PHILIPPI COLOSSUS ROME

45–90 CE Most of the New Testament is written.

41–65 CE The ministry of St Paul and others.

FURTHER ACTIVITIES

1 Look back at the Bible bookshop plan in Unit 1.

Find the shelves with the New Testament books on them. Write the names of the books in the correct sections of the bottom parts of the chart below. Use the pie chart to help you understand the bar chart.

No two people tell an identical story – unless they work it out between them first!

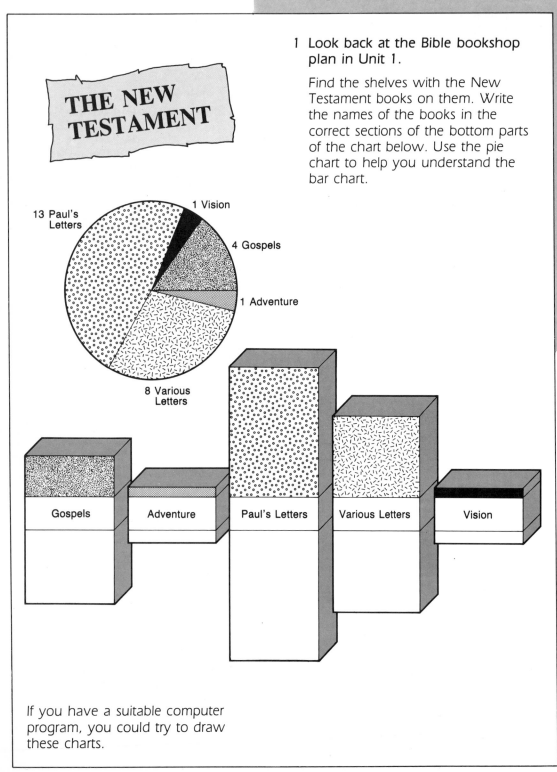

THE NEW TESTAMENT

13 Paul's Letters

1 Vision

4 Gospels

1 Adventure

8 Various Letters

Gospels | Adventure | Paul's Letters | Various Letters | Vision

If you have a suitable computer program, you could try to draw these charts.

'We always knew the big quake was coming'

e killed ferno

EX-model tells of quake nightmare.

Why don't you look at the weather on the other channel? It might be better there!

2 a In pairs

Make a quick note of what happened earlier today, when you were both together.

Now compare what you have written. If it isn't a little bit different in detail, you've been copying!

Compare notes with another pair. Have you all remembered slightly different things?

	Similarities	Differences
Matthew 3:13–17 Mark 1:9–11		

b Collect some news articles about the same news story. Make sure they are from different newspapers.
(i) What is the same in each article?
(ii) What is different in each article?

c Read carefully Matthew 3:13–17 and Mark 1:9–11.
Some of the events are the same, and some are different! Use a chart like the one below. Put all the things that are the same in the left-hand column, and the things that are different in the right-hand column.

ENCOURAGEMENT

3 Read 1 Corinthians 1:10–17.

Now use Paul's answer and, by imagining you are Paul write a helpful letter back. Make sure you give the same answer as Paul did!

12 Temple Crescent,
Corinth,
Greece,
47 C.E.

Dear Paul,

I am writing to tell you that there are some difficulties in Corinth. There are lots of quarrels. Some people say they follow you, and some of them are following Apollos or Peter. Some think they are above all the quarrels by saying they only follow Christ! Please do something about it.

Yours Tychichus
(a slave in Chloe's household).

HELP IN TROUBLED TIMES

4 People need encouragement.

What would you do to encourage
a someone housebound

b someone in hospital
c someone in prison
d someone who is fed up?

5 Much of the New Testament was written to encourage Christians who were suffering for their faith.

Some of them were imprisoned and tortured. Some were executed by crucifixion or being thrown to the lions.

Some people today are in prison for their beliefs, or for crimes which they have not committed.

a You might like to write to Amnesty International for some information about people who are imprisoned for their belief.

b Find out about Nelson Mandela who has been in prison in South Africa since 1963 because of his belief.

c Make a list of things someone would look forward to if they were in prison for a long time. Now make a similar list for someone in hospital. In what ways are the lists similar?

6 Discuss

In what ways do you think the Bible might help people who need encouragement?

7 Now read how Paul writes from prison to his friends in Colossae in Colossians 4:7–18.

a Does he sound sorry for himself?

b How can you tell from this passage that Paul is in prison?

c How does he try to encourage the Christians in Colossae?

d Do you think that Paul is getting on with his work of telling others about Jesus, even when he is in prison? Write down some reasons for your answer.

If you look again at the Bible bookshop in Unit 1, you will see that there are four **Gospels**. Three of these are quite similar. They are called the Synoptic Gospels. These are Matthew, Mark and Luke. The Fourth Gospel, John's Gospel, is rather different.

WHY WERE THE GOSPELS WRITTEN?

The main reason why the Gospels were written was to try to help people to know more about Jesus. Like Judaism, Christianity is an historical faith. It is very important for Christians to know what actually happened. They need to know about what Jesus did as well as what he said. The Synoptic Gospels are an account of what Christians believe Jesus said and did while he was on Earth.

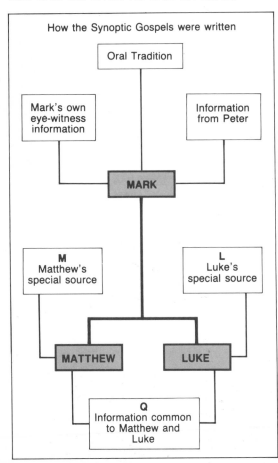

How the Synoptic Gospels were written

Oral Tradition

Mark's own eye-witness information

Information from Peter

MARK

M Matthew's special source

L Luke's special source

MATTHEW

LUKE

Q Information common to Matthew and Luke

WHEN WERE THE GOSPELS WRITTEN?

MARK

Most people think that Mark's Gospel was written first. From very early times, it has been thought that Mark knew Peter very well. Some of the events which Mark wrote about say very personal things about Peter, which probably only Peter would have known – times when he said the wrong thing or lost his temper, for example. (Look up Mark 9:5.)

Near the end of Mark's Gospel, when Jesus was arrested, there is a story about a young man who followed Jesus and the guards. He was wearing nothing but a linen cloth, and he left that behind when the guards tried to grab him. He ran away naked! (Mark 14:51.) This seems like an eye witness account. People think that this was Mark himself. He is trying to show that he was actually there, and saw what happened. Later on, Mark met Paul and Silas, and went with them on Paul's first journey. Their job on that journey was to tell other people about Jesus.

Mark probably wrote the Gospel in Rome. At the time, Christians were being **persecuted** because the Emperor Nero needed someone to take the blame for a great fire in Rome. Nero possibly started this fire himself, but he blamed the Christians so that no-one would blame him!

Mark's Gospel was written to encourage people who were being persecuted. Another reason for writing may have been the death of the first **Apostles**. At first, people thought that Jesus was coming back to Earth very soon. The Apostles were able to tell people about Jesus' life. When the Apostles got old and some of them died, it became important for Christians to have the events of the life of Jesus written down, so that the details would not be forgotten.

LUKE

Luke was a **Gentile**, or non-Jew. He may have been a doctor, and he was probably Greek. Like the other writers of the Bible, he did not know that he was writing the Bible. He simply wrote an account of the life of Jesus for a man called Theophilus (which means 'lover of God'). He was obviously writing for Gentiles, or people who were not Jews. He was also interested in writing about events which included women. He seems anxious to show the Gentile world that Jesus was prepared to allow women to be his followers on equal terms with men.

Luke went with Paul on some of his journeys. He also wrote the Acts of the Apostles. This included his own notebooks about their travels. Luke was with Paul when Paul was in prison. One of the places where Paul was in prison

A and B Two famous churches dedicated to Gospel writers

was Caesarea, on the coast of Galilee. It is thought that Luke collected a lot of information about the life of Jesus during this time. He probably knew Mary, as the stories about the birth of Jesus are told from her point of view. There are other times too when Luke seems to know a great deal about the women who followed Jesus.

MATTHEW

Matthew was probably a Jew, writing for Jews. He often quotes parts of the Old Testament. He is very interested in the occasions when Jesus fulfilled prophecy.

Luke seems to have used parts of Mark's Gospel in some of his writings. He also had some special information of his own. (We call this special information **'L'**.) There seems to have been another account of the life of Jesus around at the time as well. This is now lost. It seems to have been used by Matthew as well as Luke. We call this source **'Q'**. Matthew also seems to have had some special information of his own. (We call this special information **'M'**.)

Look carefully at the diagram of how the Synoptic Gospels were written to help you understand how the Gospel writers used information from several different sources.

JOHN

John's Gospel, or the Fourth Gospel, is very different. John is more interested in the meaning of what Jesus said and did than in the events themselves. This was possibly written later than the other Gospels, and possibly by the John who was one of Jesus's first **disciples**.

Together, the Four Gospels tell us a lot about the events of the life, death and **Resurrection** of Jesus. They have helped Christians throughout history to find meaning in their own lives.

NOTES/DATABASE

Use the glossary to look up the meanings of the following words. Then use the definitions to make your own notes or suitable entries on your database.

Gospel   Gentile

Persecuted   Disciple

Apostle   Resurrection

ACTIVITIES

ADVENTURE IN THE DARK

"Mark became the interpreter for Peter, and he wrote down accurately the things which Peter remembered about what the Lord had said and done. He did not, however, write them in the correct order." *(Papias, a second century bishop.)*

1 Read carefully the story about the young man who ran away naked.

(You will need to use Mark 14:51f.)

Now imagine that you were the young man. You were probably hiding in the bushes, having sneaked out at night without your parents knowing.

Write a letter to a school friend describing what you did that night. Say what happened to Jesus, as well as describing the trouble you would have got into if your parents had found out!

C Greeks had a very different outlook on life. For example, they loved athletics

2 Quick quiz

a Write down the names of the first three Gospels.

b What is the special name which these Gospels have?

c Why were the Gospels written?

d Which Gospel was written first?

e Why do people think Mark knew Peter?

f Who was the young man who ran away naked?

g What did Mark do later?

h Why were Christians blamed for the fire in Rome?

i Why were the events of the life of Jesus not written down earlier?

j What did Luke do for a living?

k When did Luke collect his special information?

l What other book did Luke write?

m Who did Luke write his book for?

n Who wrote a Gospel for Jews to read?

o Why is John's Gospel different?

INTRODUCING LUKE . . . WRITER, TRAVELLER AND DOCTOR

1 Many books today are dedicated to people. Look inside a few books and find a dedication. Usually they read something like this:

To my daughter Elizabeth, for being so wonderful and helpful while I wrote this book.

If you were writing a book, how would you dedicate it? Write down some of your ideas.

FURTHER ACTIVITIES

2 **To Theophilus: read Luke 1:1–4.**

This is Luke's dedication of his book.

a Who is Luke dedicating his book to?

b Are there any other books which have already been written on the same subject?

c Why is Luke so sure that his account is accurate?

d Who collected the information in the book?

e What was the main reason for Luke writing his book?

INTRODUCING MATTHEW . . . A JEWISH WRITER

4 Be honest! When you have a project do do, how much do you copy from books? If you had to find out about Julius Caesar what would you do?

Work out a survey similar to the one below to find out how people research their information.

A Visit
   a school library ☐
   b town library ☐
   c your own bookshelf. ☐

B Ask:
   a adult at home ☐
   b teacher ☐
   c another pupil. ☐

C a photocopy article ☐
   b copy out some of the article ☐
   c write the article in your own words ☐

If your answer shows that you copy out chunks from other books and add bits of your own in-between, then your methods are just like Matthew's. There are 661 verses in Mark, and Matthew copied 606 of them.

3

LETTERS TO THE EDITOR

Hillel ben Abraham,
Pharisee's House,
Capernaum.

Dear Editor,
I am disgusted to hear that this self-appointed Rabbi, Jesus of Nazareth, has been healing Romans! Surely this shows he cannot be a good Jew. Under our law he cannot possibly heal a Roman. Even more appalling, it was a mere servant that he bothered to heal. This unnecessary showing off of his power to heal can only lead to Jesus getting himself in trouble with the religious authorities. It is not proper for Jews to have anything to do with Romans.

Yours,
Disgusted.

a Write a letter to the editor replying to the above letter. Make sure you use all the real facts from Luke 7:1–10.

Luke's writings tell us about his personality.

Luke is interested in the underdog. He writes about occasions when Jesus helped people who were not Jews, for example Luke 7:1–10. Read this story yourself to find out what happened.

Luke told the story of the Good Samaritan as well. Jews did not like Samaritans. Jewish law said that they were not to mix with foreigners. Most Jews would not even eat a meal in the house of someone who was not a Jew.

b (i) Why do you think Luke (who was Greek) includes lots of stories about foreigners who met Jesus?
(ii) Why do you think Luke (who might have been a slave) included lots of stories about people who were usually badly treated, but were helped by Jesus?

How can we find out what Matthew was specially interested in?

By looking at the bits he specially adds which he didn't copy from Mark!

5 Matthew is interested in the Church, for example Matthew 16:18, "You are Peter and on this rock I will build my church."

Matthew is very interested in telling about what Jesus said to help people live a Christian life (Matthew 5–7).

These verses are very famous. We call this the Sermon on the Mount. Let's have a closer look at a bit of it. Choose one of the following sections:

A Matthew 5:43

a What was the old rule?

b What is Jesus' new rule?

c Does God make differences between people?

d Do you think Jesus would expect you to be kind only to people who were kind to you? Write down some reasons for your answer.

B Matthew 6:1–4

a Why do you think Jesus didn't want people to show off about how religious they were?

b How does Jesus suggest people should give to charity?

c What do you think about well-known people letting the world know how much they give to a good cause?

d Look up verse 3. Do you agree with Jesus?

INTRODUCING JOHN . . . ONE OF JESUS' CLOSEST FRIENDS

6 **John**

a Look back at the Bible bookshop in Unit 1 and find out which other books in the New Testament were written by John.

b Look at John 1:1–14 and 1 John 1:1–9.
Make a list of the important words which appear in each section. John is always interested in the meaning of everything Jesus said and did.

JOHN'S KEY WORDS

Love
Light
the Word
Life

7 Now read John 15:11–17.

a What does Jesus want his disciples to do?

b What is the greatest kind of love?

c How were the disciples expected to show that they were Jesus' friends?

d What is the most loving thing anyone has ever done for you?

e What is the most loving thing you have ever done for anyone else?

PROFILE ON JOHN

Name: *John, son of Zebedee*

Born: *Capernaum*

Address: *no fixed abode*

Relations: *brother James (executed CE 30 in Jerusalem)*

Trade: *fisherman*

Other details: *He became a follower of Jesus when only a teenager and was Jesus' closest friend. He looked after Mary, Jesus' mother, after the death of Jesus. Often called 'the disciple Jesus loved best'. He went with Jesus when Jesus healed Jairus' daughter and when he was transfigured (changed) on the mountain. He was there at the Crucifixion. Later John was a leader of the Church, wrote the Gospel and Letters, and was imprisoned for being a Christian on the island of Patmos where he wrote the book of Revelation.*

At the beginning of his **ministry**, Jesus chose twelve men to follow him. After his death and **Resurrection** eleven of them remained, and they became known as **Apostles**. The word 'apostle' means 'someone sent out with an important message'. This message changed the course of history.

After Jesus returned to his father, the first thing the eleven decided to do was to hold an election for a twelfth apostle. They wanted to replace Judas. They chose Matthias, who had been with them from the beginning. They were ready for the next part of the adventure.

THE APOSTLES

The Apostles knew what their job was to be. This is what Jesus had told them:

"Go, then, to all nations, everywhere in the world, and make them my **disciples**: **baptize** them in the name of the Father, the Son and the Holy Spirit. Teach them to obey everything I have commanded you. And I will always be with you, until the end of time."
(Matthew 28:19)

Before he left them, Jesus promised the Apostles special power to help them to actually do this. This is what he said:

"When the Holy Spirit comes to you, you will be filled with power. You will tell people about me in Jerusalem, in Judea, in Samaria, and all over the world."
(Acts 1:8)

The rest of the New Testament is the record of how they did this.

The Acts of the Apostles is perhaps one of the most exciting real-life adventure stories which has ever been written. The Apostles certainly could not have expected the dangerous life they would lead when they left home to follow Jesus. They thought they were just the disciples of a wandering **rabbi**.

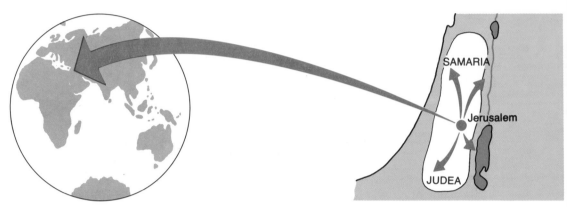

"Tell people about me in Jerusalem, Judea, Samaria, and throughout the rest of the world"
Acts 1:8

Little did they know that within a few years they would be taking the teachings of that wandering rabbi all over the world. They could never have expected to be telling people who were not **Jews** about God and about Jesus.

PAUL

Soon there was another Apostle, named Paul. He had been a very strict Jew, and had put Christians in prison for their beliefs. Read the story of how he became a Christian in Acts 9. He went on several journeys all over the world to tell people about Jesus. His adventures can be found in the Acts of the Apostles.

The Apostles would visit a city and tell people about Jesus. They would stay in that city for a while, teaching the people. Then they would appoint local leaders to look after the Christians in that place, and would move on somewhere else to tell more people about Jesus.

LETTER WRITING

They needed to try to keep in touch with the **Church** and to help the new followers of Jesus. This was why the Apostles wrote letters to the churches. They probably wrote many more letters than we actually have now. We can find some of the letters which they wrote in the second part of the New Testament. There are more letters by Paul than by anyone else. There are also letters by Peter (one of Jesus' first disciples) and by John (Jesus' closest friend), and by James and Jude who seem to have been Jesus' brothers. John also wrote a book called Revelation.

People today write letters for all sorts of reasons, and in the New Testament it was just the same. Paul wrote to encourage the churches which he had started. He also wrote to give them good advice when things went wrong, and sometimes to tell them off. On one occasion he wrote a letter to someone

At first, letters were carried by hand... ...until there were too many. ...then the horse carried them.

Later on, they needed to put the mail on coaches, but this was often slow.

So they tried trains, aeroplanes, satellites and even carrier pigeons!

Now, of cours we can send important thing instantly by computer or even Fax.

called Philemon whose slave had run away. When Paul met the slave and sent him home to Philemon, he wrote a letter to try and sort the situation out.

Peter wrote a letter to encourage Christians who were being **persecuted**. It seems to have been for a special occasion, a baptism, when new members would join the Church.

The New Testament letters were written for a special purpose. They show us what kind of problems people were encountering as they began to live Christian lives, and how the Apostles tried to help and give good advice.

Christians today meet the same kind of problems and difficulties. They often find that the New Testament letters help to provide answers to today's problems, just as they did when they were first written.

NOTES/DATABASE

Use the glossary to look up the meanings of the following words. Then use the definitions to make your own notes or suitable entries on your database.

Ministry	Rabbi
Resurrection	Jews
Apostle	Church
Disciple	Persecuted
Baptize	

2 a Copy the map into your books.

 b Place a tick beside any places you can find on the map to which Paul wrote a letter.

People had an unusual way of starting letters in those days. Read Romans 1:1 and 1 Corinthians 1:1. Now imagine you are writing a letter then. Write down how you would begin.

ACTIVITIES

1 Quick quiz

a How many disciples did Jesus choose to follow him?

b What is an Apostle?

c What was the first thing the Apostles decided to do after Jesus returned to his father?

d Who replaced Judas?

e In your own words, explain what the job of the Apostles was.

f What did Jesus promise the Apostles to help them carry out their job?

g Describe how Paul became a Christian.

h Why do you think the Apostles appointed local leaders in the cities before they moved on?

i Why did the Apostles write letters to the churches?

j Where can we find some of the letters which the Apostles wrote?

k Name some of the Apostles whose letters we can still read today.

l Write down some of the things which Paul wrote about to encourage the churches.

m What did Peter write about?

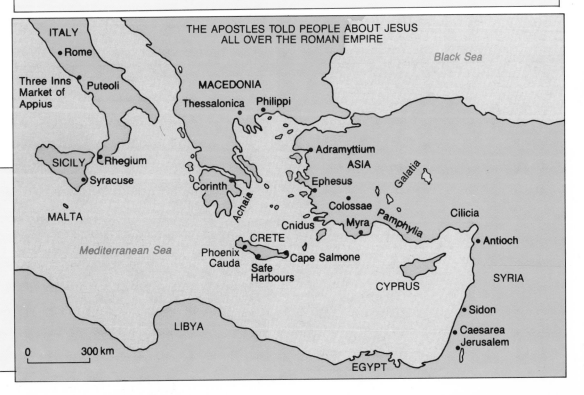

THE APOSTLES TOLD PEOPLE ABOUT JESUS ALL OVER THE ROMAN EMPIRE

FURTHER ACTIVITIES

I'D LIKE TO RETURN YOUR PROPERTY!

1 In the time of Paul, slaves were objects which could be bought and sold. Sometimes they ran away. Sometimes they were burnt with an iron to show who owned them.

Read the letter to Philemon.

a Do you think Philemon was a Christian?

b What was the slave's name?

c Do you think Paul liked Philemon? Write down some reasons for your answer.

d Where was Paul when he wrote this letter?

e Who was with Paul?

f What do you think Paul means when he calls Onesimus "my son in Christ"?

g Why do you think Paul would like to keep Onesimus?

Following the Safe Arrival of the "Sea Witch"

A Grand Sale of 296 Slaves.
All in Prime condition, including 125 Healthy Bucks and at least 30 Women with Child.
Replenish your Plantations at the Forthcoming Auction.

h Why does Paul say Onesimus is now Philemon's brother?

i How does Paul try to make it easier for Onesimus to return (verses 17–20)?

j What else does Paul want Philemon to do for him?

4 The reasons why Paul and the other Apostles wrote letters are not so very different from the reasons people write letters today. The chart on this page lists some of the reasons why the Apostles wrote letters, and asks you to find out why people now write letters.

a Use a chart like the one below to conduct a survey of your friends or family to help you find out the reasons why they write letters.

b Collect the numbers of people who write letters for different reasons.

c Now display your findings in a bar chart.

2 Discuss

Paul is obviously so used to some people being slaves, that he does not think it wrong. Why do you think Christians now think slavery is wrong?

3 Find out . . .

about the Slave Trade and the way it was stopped. See if you can find out about William Wilberforce and the way he helped stop slavery.

Reason	Number
a To say thank you for a present or visit etc.	
b To ask for advice.	
c In answer to someone who has asked for advice.	
d To ask someone to do something for you.	
e To explain why you did something.	
f To return someone's property which you borrowed.	
g To encourage someone who was ill or in prison.	
h To complain about something.	
i To praise someone for something they have done.	
j To ask someone to send something to you.	
k Business letters.	

LIVING DANGEROUSLY

This is what some very religious people said to the chief priests:

> We have promised not to eat a single thing until we have killed Paul! (Acts 23:14)

5 a What could he have done to deserve it?

  Find out Paul's version by reading Acts 22:1–21.

 b Now note what the people said in verse 22.

 c Imagine that you had been one of the people in the crowd. Write a newspaper report which explains what Paul said that day. The one on this page will give you some extra information.

IF YOU ARE A SNOB DON'T READ THIS!

6 The letter from James

Saying the right things is not enough – you have to behave in the right way too!

James 2:1–4

"My brothers! In your life as believers in our Lord Jesus Christ, the Lord of glory, you must never treat people in different ways because of their outward appearance. Suppose a rich man wearing a gold ring and fine clothes comes into your meeting, and a poor man in ragged clothes also comes in. If you show more respect to the well-dressed man and say to him, 'Have this best seat here', but say to the poor man, 'Stand or sit down here on the floor by my seat', then you are guilty of creating distinctions among yourselves and making judgments based on evil motives."

This is a very common situation. Make up a story in which something similar happens. Imagine you are the poor person who arrived, and explain how you felt about the way you are treated compared with the rich person.

7 Something to think about

Christians believe that everyone has the right to be treated equally.

 a How can Christians try to make sure that they treat poor people (wherever they live) and rich people equally?

 b Do you think that Church leaders have the right to live in 'posh' houses while other people are homeless? Can they do anything positive to make things more equal?

Jerusalem Times 58 CE

The notorious Paul of Tarsus was arrested yesterday. He dared to come into the Temple with four men who had taken a special vow not to cut their hair.

Paul, a former student here in Jerusalem, believes that he has a right to enter the Temple because he says he is a good Jew. Others would argue that he spends so much time with Gentiles (non-Jews) that he is no longer a strict enough Jew to have the right to come into the Temple. He has been telling Gentiles that they can believe in the God of Israel and have all the privileges God gives to Jews simply by believing in Jesus of Nazareth. This Jesus was crucified here in Jerusalem about 30 years ago. There have been persistent rumours that he came alive again and was seen in Jerusalem for six weeks after his death.

Paul is criticized by the Jewish religious authorities for believing in Jesus. Paul is being held and questioned by the Romans. Jewish authorities hope he will be dealt with very severely.

Jesus was a **Jew**. The God he spoke about was the same one that we meet in the pages of the Old Testament. God does not change. Everything we know about God from the Old Testament is true also of the God of the New Testament. The God of the New Testament is one God. When Jesus was asked what the most important part of faith was, he replied in the words of Deuteronomy 6:4,

"The Lord your God is one Lord and you shall love the Lord your God with all your heart and with all your soul and with all your mind and with all your strength."

Again in the words of the Old Testament Jesus added, "and you shall love your neighbour as much as you love yourself."

This is the central part of what the New Testament teaches us about God, and it is basically the same as the Old Testament message. There is one God who loves his people, and he expects his people both to love him, and to love other people. The way they show that they love God is by obedience to the things he wants them to do. What he wants them to do was put very clearly by the prophet Micah:

"You shall do justly, love mercy and walk humbly with your God."

In other words, the God of the Old Testament, who is also the God of the New Testament, wants his people to treat other people with love, kindness and respect. If they do this, then they show that they love and worship God.

Jesus explained what God was like by calling him 'father'. He shocked some of the strict Jews by using the **Aramaic** word which meant 'daddy'. This word is **'abba'** and is used even now by Hebrew and Arab children when they speak to their own father.

When Jesus used the word 'abba' about God, he upset people. They thought that by using this word, he was claiming to be equal with God. Jesus said that it was the way everyone should think of God. God loves his people in the way the best of fathers loves his children. Everyone, Jesus said, should know that that was how God felt about them, and

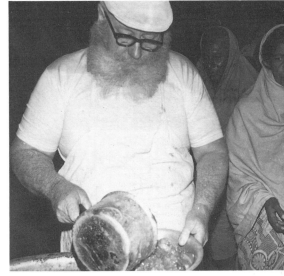

C A Salvation Army Officer

should talk to God, calling him Father. They should expect him to treat them in the way that a good father treats his children.

In the Old Testament God was someone who actually did things to direct the course of history. He was always interested in his people and

B Prior Roger Schutz in the church at Taizé

A Prior Roger Schutz and a Vietnamese girl who lives at Taizé

D Jesus said God is like a father

always with them. He led and guided them throughout their history. In the New Testament God is presented in exactly the same way. He leads and guides his people. He actually got involved in history by becoming human in Jesus Christ. He is always present with his people. He is always reliable, and gives his people whatever is best for them.

"God is Love", the New Testament says. This does not mean that God is not also just. There are occasions in the New Testament when God is described as a Judge. He is always presented as a fair judge, but there are times when fair judges have to punish people, and this is part of the nature of God as well.

It is a central part of the Christian religion (and of the Jewish religion) that God is always good.

NOTES/DATABASE

Use the glossary to look up the meanings of the following words. Then use the definitions to make your own notes or suitable entries on your database.

Jew Abba

Aramaic

ACTIVITIES

1 Quick quiz

a Why do Christians believe that the God of the New Testament is one God?

b How do the people show that they love God?

c How does the God of the Old Testament and the God of the New Testament want his people to treat other people?

d What did Jesus call God?

e Why did Jesus call him this?

f Why were the strict Jews shocked when Jesus used the Aramaic word?

g How did Jesus say the people should expect God, the Father, to treat his children?

h What sort of a judge is God?

i What do you think has helped Christians to cope with every kind of difficulty?

2 Now look at Luke 11:1–4.

This is how Jesus told people they should pray.

a What is God called in this prayer?

b Do you think it helps Christians to think of God as father?

c Write a prayer of your own beginning 'Father'.

d Make a collection of hymns which you sing in assembly in which God is called 'Father'.

GOD THE FATHER

Jesus was often asked, "What is God like?" One of the ways in which he explained was by saying that God was like a good father.

3 Discuss

If you ask your dad for a fish, what do you expect him to give you?
If you ask him for an egg, what would you usually expect to get?

4 Read Luke 11:11–13.

How did Jesus use the questions above to help explain what God is like?

FURTHER ACTIVITIES

THE WASTER!

1 Using Luke 15:11–32, complete the story, either in your own words or by drawing some more pictures

2 a Why do you think the boy wanted his share of the money at that time?

b How do you think he felt when all he could get to eat was pig food?

c What do you think he planned to say to his dad?

d How do you think his dad felt all the time he was away?

e When the boy returned home, how do you think his father felt then?

Jesus said God is like the father in this story.

God the Father goes on loving and wanting his children to be with him, even when they have chosen to turn away from him.

Like the father in the story, Jesus said, he is always ready to welcome his children home again.

How does God feel?

3 How do you think God feels about each of these pictures?

4 Things good fathers do!

Copy and complete the chart below by making a list in Column A of the things you would expect a good father to do. Put a tick against the things you would expect God to do

A Human father	B God the Father
Love his children	

if he were like a good father. If there are any extra ones to add in Column B, put them in.

God the Father is always a loving father, but a loving father sometimes has to discipline his children.

THE WORKERS IN THE VINEYARD

How about turning this into a play!

Read Matthew 20:1–16.

5 Discuss

a Do you think it is a good idea to be paid exactly for the amount of work you do?

b Everyone in the country needs the same minimum wage to live on. What do you think of the suggestion that because everyone needs the same, everyone should be paid the same?

c (i) What do you think Jesus would think of the enormous differences in the amount of money people in the rich northern nations have compared with the poorer southern nations? (ii) What can people do to try and fit in better with what Jesus would have wanted?

Make a list in a chart like the one below. Tick off the ones you could make a start on. The list has been started for you. Now see how many things you can add.

Things we can do	I could do this
Write a letter to your MP. Find out about Christian Aid.	

The New Testament leaves us in no doubt about the basic facts of the life, death and Resurrection of Jesus Christ. It also tells us what the Early Church believed about him. This belief is identical to what Christians believe about Jesus today.

Jesus, whose Hebrew name was Joshua, was born in Galilee in about the year 6 BCE. He was the son of a poor Galilean girl called Mary. He was conceived before his parents were properly married, and his earthly father's name was Joseph. He was called Jesus because the name means 'saviour' and Joseph was told in a dream before Jesus was born that Jesus would 'save his people from their sins'.

Jesus lived most of his early life in total obscurity. We only know one thing about his childhood. This is the time when he went with his parents to Jerusalem, possibly for the coming of age ceremony, now known as **bar mitzvah**.

During the journey home the boy, aged about twelve, was found to be missing, and his worried parents searched Jerusalem for him. They eventually found him three days later. He was in the Temple! Read the story for yourself. You will find it in Luke 2:41–51.

Jesus did not start to tell people about God or to gather a group of followers until he was about thirty years old. Then, after being baptized, he spent three years wandering all over Israel teaching people about God and about himself.

Some of the claims which Jesus made for himself, and later on his followers made for him, are extraordinary. The group of followers, called disciples in the New Testament, lived with him, slept alongside him, ate with him, and shared

B Jesus preaching

A Jesus in the Temple

every aspect of his life. And yet, despite having seen him as very human, they still claimed that this man was the Son of God.

On one occasion, the disciples were asked who they thought he was. Simon Peter replied, "You are the Christ, the Son of the Living God." This is an enormous claim to make about someone they knew so well. They continued to make this claim when they were imprisoned and were even put to death for saying it.

Shortly after this, Jesus was arrested. His trial was a mockery, and in the hastily gathered court he was condemned to death. The Romans were the only people with the right to put a man to death, so the Jews produced some trumped-up charges on which he was convicted.

He was executed by being crucified like a common criminal. This was perhaps the most degrading and humiliating form of execution which has ever been devised. The way in which he submitted to the death penalty impressed one of the Roman officers so much that he became a believer in Jesus whilst Jesus was still dying.

Jesus was buried in a tomb borrowed from a rich man called Joseph of Arimathea. Three days later he was reported alive again and he continued to appear to his disciples for forty days.

Soon the disciples began to make sense of what had happened. They saw his death on the Cross as an incredible victory. It was the victory of good over evil. Jesus, they claimed, was the Son of God. He was the Messiah who Jews had long awaited. He was the person that God used to make it possible for everyone to know God for themselves, and to be accepted by God. His death was not the end, it was only a beginning. His death on the Cross meant that people who believed in him were set free to live a new kind of life. In this new kind of life, they could be absolutely certain that God had forgiven all their sins. The disciples went out into the world with this message:

"Our message is, that God was making all mankind his friends through Christ . . . Christ was without sin, but for our sake, God made him share our sin in order that in union with him we might share the righteousness of God."
(2 Corinthians 5:19ff)

NOTES/DATABASE

Use the glossary to look up the meaning of the following word. Then use the definition to make your own notes or suitable entry on your database.

Bar mitzvah

C The Crucifixion

D Salvador Dali's painting of the Crucifixion

ACTIVITIES

1 **Quick quiz**

a What are the main facts the New Testament tells us about?

b What was the Hebrew name for Jesus?

c Where was Jesus born?

d What does the name Jesus mean?

e What do we know about Jesus' childhood?

f Jesus went missing when he was a young boy. Where was he found?

g When Jesus spent three years wandering all over Israel, what did Jesus teach the people?

h Why were some of the claims made by Jesus and his disciples extraordinary?

i Why did the Jews make charges against Jesus?

j How was Jesus executed?

k Why did one of the Roman officers become a believer in Jesus while Jesus was dying?

l Who was the tomb for Jesus borrowed from?

m How long after his death was Jesus seen again?

n Why was Jesus' death on the Cross seen as a victory?

JERUSALEM TIMES

ASTOUNDING CLAIMS MADE FOR DEAD REBEL

The leader of the rebel group who were the followers of Jesus of Nazareth are refusing to give up even when their leader is dead. We quote exactly what their leader, an uneducated fisherman from Galilee, said about him.

Acts 2:22–24
"Listen to these words, men of Israel! Jesus of Nazareth was a man whose divine mission was clearly shown to you by the miracles, wonders, and signs which God did through him; you yourselves know this, for it took place among you. God, in his own will and knowledge, had already decided that Jesus would be handed over to you; and you killed him, by letting sinful men nail him to the cross. But God raised him from the dead; he set him free from the pains of death, for it was impossible that death should hold him prisoner."

This summarizes the early Christian belief in Jesus. Other speeches in Acts contain exactly the same details. This is the basic truth of Christianity.

1 Now try to turn Peter's speech into a list of points.

The first few are done for you.

a	Jesus of Nazareth was a man who got his authority from God.
b	He carried out miracles, wonders and signs.
c	
d	

2 Draw a series of pictures to illustrate the points in your list.

Here are some Bible references, in the correct order, which may help you.

(i) Mark 1:11
(ii) John 2:1–10
(iii) Mark 14:43
(iv) Mark 15:25
(v) Mark 16:9

JESUS WAS CALLED

a Messiah

Messiah is a Hebrew word meaning 'anointed one'. The Greek word is Christ. It means the same. Although Jesus accepted the title 'Messiah', he was very cautious about people using it. The people thought that the Messiah was a king. They once tried making him King by force.

b Son of Man

This was Jesus' favourite way of talking about himself.

The phrase could mean (i) 'human beings' or (ii) 'son of Adam' – an ordinary Jewish surname, or (iii) simply a very humble way of talking about yourself instead of saying 'I' or 'me'; or (iv) a title for the Messiah, used in Daniel 7:13–14.

It annoyed the Jewish leaders at Jesus' trial. This is what he said when asked if he was the Messiah:

"I am . . . and you will all see the Son of Man seated on the right hand of the Almighty and coming with the clouds of heaven."
(Mark 14:62)

c Son of God

When Jesus was a boy, he was aware of a special relationship with God. This is what he said when he was about twelve:

"Didn't you know I had to be in my Father's House?"
(Luke 2:49)

Later on, when Jesus was baptized, he heard a voice saying, "You are my son, I love you and I am pleased with you." (Mark 1:11). He taught everyone to call God 'Father'. He wanted them to have the same kind of relationship with God as he had. In fact, it was Jesus who made that kind of relationship possible for everyone else.

d The Lord

This was what the Christians started calling Jesus after the Resurrection. 'The Lord' was a polite way of speaking to someone. It meant 'Sir' (Greek: – κυριος kurios). It was also used to translate the word used for God (adonai – יהוה) in the Old Testament. By using this word, Jewish people were saying Jesus was in fact God.

JESUS AND THE NEW TESTAMENT

3 Some questions to answer

a What does the word 'Messiah' mean?

b What Greek word means the same?

c Why do you think Jesus was cautious about people using the title 'Messiah'?

d What was Jesus' favourite way of talking about himself?

e What are the three different things this title could mean?

f Why do you think it annoyed the Jewish leaders at his trial?

g How do we know that Jesus was aware of a special relationship with God when he was still a boy?

h What sign was Jesus given that God was really with him when he was baptized?

i Why did he want everyone to call God 'Father'?

j What did Greek-speaking Jews call God?

k What did Christians start to call Jesus after the Resurrection?

l How did the use of the word 'kurios' show that people thought Jesus was God?

4 Imagine you had to write a short speech explaining who Jesus was.

Either:

a Write down your speech, or:

b record your speech.

5 The list of things which Peter said in his speech is identical to what Christians now (and all through history) believe about Jesus.

Find out what people believe about Jesus.

Use a survey form like the one below with several people, and then draw a series of bar charts to display your results.

E 'Christ in Majesty', Rio de Janeiro

SURVEY FORM

Question	Yes	No	Don't know
a Do you think school pupils should learn about Jesus?			
b Do you think Jesus was sent by God?			
c Do you think Jesus worked miracles?			
d Do you think he should have been executed?			
e Do you think he rose again from the dead?			
f Do you think he was the Son of God?			
g Do you think he changed the course of history?			
h Do you think he can still change peoples' lives?			
i Any other comments . . .			

The Holy Spirit is never explained in the New Testament. It is always assumed that readers will understand who the Holy Spirit is because they would have read the Old Testament or because of their own personal experience of the Holy Spirit. Put very simply, the Holy Spirit, in the New Testament, is the power of God at work. When God wants to accomplish something on Earth, he does it by using the Holy Spirit.

When the angel Gabriel told Mary that she was going to have a baby who was to be the Messiah, Mary asked a question. "How can that happen?" she said. "I'm not married." The angel told her, "The Holy Spirit will come on you and God's power will overshadow you." (Luke 1:35). Soon after this Mary visited her cousin Elizabeth, and, the Bible says, Elizabeth was filled with the Holy Spirit which helped her to know what a special person Jesus was going to be (Luke 1:41). Similarly, Zechariah, after the birth of John the Baptist, was said to be "full of the Holy Spirit" (Luke 1:67).

So it seems that in the New Testament, the Holy Spirit gives people special extra

A The Annunciation

knowledge or information. This is very similar to what happened in the Old Testament.

From the very beginning of the **ministry**, the Holy Spirit was expected to be involved in the work of Jesus. In Mark 1:8, John says that when the Messiah comes, he will be different because he will baptize people with the Holy Spirit instead of with water. After Jesus was baptized, the Holy Spirit, it is said, "descended upon him like a dove". It was the Holy Spirit which then led Jesus away into the desert for forty days.

Throughout his ministry, the Holy Spirit was present with Jesus. When he preached his sermon in the **synagogue** at Nazareth, he chose a part of the Old Testament which referred to the Holy Spirit to show everyone that he believed that he was the Messiah. (Remind yourself of the story by looking at Luke 4:16ff.)

Whenever baptism is mentioned in the New Testament, it seems to be clearly linked, as it was by John the Baptist, with the gift of the Holy Spirit. If you look at Peter's speech to the people of Jerusalem (Acts 2:38), you will see how Peter links baptism and the gift of the Spirit. The Holy Spirit seems to be given to people at their baptism to help them to live the kind of life Jesus wants them to, and also to help them to tell other people about Jesus.

Before he was crucified, Jesus told the disciples more about the Holy Spirit. This time he called it the **'paraclete'** (John 14:26). Some translations of the Bible use the word 'helper' to translate this word. Others use 'comforter', 'counsellor', or 'advocate'. It really means a mixture of all these things. Try using a variety of different translations of the Bible to see which word each uses. See how many different translations you can collect. They will all be right, and each one will help you to know a little more of what Jesus meant when he promised that the Holy Spirit would be with his disciples.

In Acts 1:8 it is quite clear that the reason for the gift of the Holy Spirit is to help the disciples to tell other people about Jesus, not just in Jerusalem but all over the world.

The promise of the Holy Spirit is fulfilled in Acts 2, on the Day of **Pentecost**. This was a feast day in Israel and people from all over the world were in Jerusalem. That day, they all heard the message about Jesus in their own languages and were able to return to their own countries and tell others about Jesus. The gift of the Spirit was really the Church's birthday present. It enabled the disciples to go all over the world to tell others about Jesus, and to be sure that he was always with them to help them and encourage them.

NOTES/DATABASE

Use the glossary to look up the meanings of the following words. Then use the definitions to make your own notes or suitable entries on your database.

Ministry	Pentecost
Synagogue	Confirmation
Paraclete	

B The temptations of Christ

ACTIVITIES

1 Quick quiz

a Why does the New Testament never explain what the Holy Spirit is?

b What is a simple explanation of the Holy Spirit?

c In what way was the Holy Spirit important in the story of the birth of Jesus?

d Write down the names of two people who were given special information by the Holy Spirit.

e What did John the Baptist say about the way the Messiah would baptize people?

f How does the Bible say that the Holy Spirit was present at the baptism of Jesus?

g Why do you think that Jesus referred to the Holy Spirit when he preached in the synagogue at Nazareth?

h How did Peter link baptism and the Holy Spirit in his speech in Acts 2:38?

i What did Jesus promise to his disciples to help them when he was no longer with them (John 14:26)?

j What is the main reason for the gift of the Holy Spirit?

k What was the name of the Jewish feast day on which the promise of the Spirit was fulfilled?

l What enabled the disciples to go all over the world to tell people about Jesus?

GO INTO ALL THE WORLD . . .

2 Read Acts 2 and then answer these questions.

a How many disciples were in the upper room?

b After the Resurrection, Jesus appeared to 500 disciples all at once. He told the disciples to wait in Jerusalem for the Holy Spirit to come. How many of the disciples did not do as they were told?

c How did the disciples know that the Spirit had come?

d How did the disciples behave differently after they were filled with the Holy Spirit?

e What did Peter tell everyone else to do so they could also receive the gift of the Spirit (verse 38)?

On this page are some banners which churches have made to help people understand more about the gift of the Spirit. Look carefully at the pictures, and then design your own banner which explains the gift of the Spirit. You might like to make this yourself as an appliqué or a collage.

C Banners of the Holy Spirit: modern Church embroidery

FURTHER ACTIVITIES

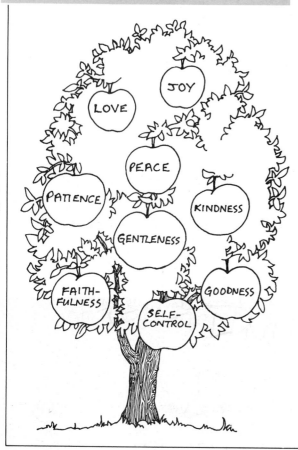

THE FRUIT OF THE SPIRIT

1 Read Galatians 5:22.

a Draw your own 'Spirit tree' full of fruit.

b Use the list in Galatians 5:22f to complete the names of the fruit of the spirit on your drawing.

c Why do you think Paul says there can be no law against any of these?

d Tick off which of the qualities shown in Column A you think you have by placing a tick in Column B. Then in Column C show which qualities you would like to have.

A Fruit of the Spirit	B Qualities I have	C Qualities I would like to have
Love		
Joy		
Peace		
Patience		
Kindness		
Goodness		
Faithfulness		
Gentleness		
Self-control		

GIFTS OF THE SPIRIT

2 Read Romans 12:3–8 and 1 Corinthians 12:4–10.

The gifts in the parcels are the gifts of the Spirit.

a List the correct gifts in each column of the chart.

b Should everyone expect to have all of these gifts?

c Look back at your chart. Place a tick next to the gifts which you think you have.

Romans 12:3–8	1 Corinthians 12:4–10	Gifts which I have

d Something to think about
(i) How should you use the gifts you have been given?

(ii) Are your gifts just for you or should you be learning to use them to help others?

PAUL IN EPHESUS

D Ephesus

3 Read the story in Acts 19:1–10 (the Holy Spirit and the laying on of hands).

In a small group, use the story as the basis of a script for a play. Act out what your group think happened.

Now:

4 What do you think the newspapers would have made of these strange events?

Either

a Write a newspaper article about this event.

Or

b Write a letter to the newspaper explaining what happened.

You could pretend to be one of the people who was baptized, or someone who was watching, or even someone who had heard the story from someone else!

Links with today!

Perhaps someone in your class has been confirmed. This story in Acts 19:1–10 is often read out at confirmations.

Confirmation is the second half of baptism, when people make the promises for themselves which their parents had made for them when they were baptized as babies. The Bishop puts his hands on their heads as a sign that they have received the gift of the Holy Spirit.

5 a **Something to think about**

Why do you think that this story (Acts 19:1–10) is often chosen as the reading for a Confirmation Service?

b **Find out . . .**

Everything you can about a Confirmation Service. You might like to invite your local vicar or parish priest to tell you about Confirmation. Some people in your class may have been confirmed. Encourage them to tell you about the service.

E A confirmation

After the first disciples had received the gift of the Holy Spirit, they started to tell other people all about Jesus. Many people in Jerusalem became believers in Jesus. At first, they were well respected in Jerusalem because they looked after the poor people. They tried to make sure that everyone had enough food and clothing, and somewhere to live.

However, their popularity didn't last. Soon some of the Jewish religious leaders began to object to the followers of Jesus. They began to be persecuted. That means being punished for their belief in Jesus. Some of them fled to a town called Antioch. Many people in Antioch also became believers in Jesus.

CHRISTIANS

It was in Antioch that the **believers** were called 'Christians' for the first time (Acts 11:26). This was obviously such a good name for the believers in Jesus that the name stuck and it is still used today.

JEWS AND GENTILES

At first, most of the Christians were also Jews. The Church was really a group of people within the Jewish religion who believed all the same things as the rest of the Jews as well as believing in Jesus.

Soon, the Church had to face the problem of people who were not Jews who wanted to become believers in Jesus. One of the first of these was a Roman soldier called Cornelius. You can read about him, and how Peter was persuaded to accept him as a Christian, in Acts 10.

People who are not Jews are Gentiles. Another Gentile who became one of the first Christians was an important Ethiopian official. He became a believer in Jesus whilst travelling in a chariot across the Judean desert, and was baptized immediately. His story is in Acts 8.

A The Colosseum

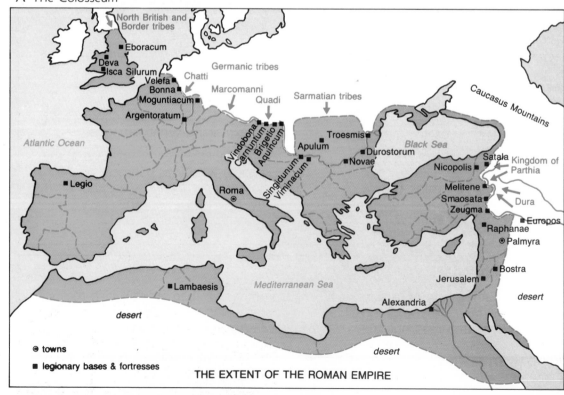

THE EXTENT OF THE ROMAN EMPIRE

⊚ towns

■ legionary bases & fortresses

CREEDS

People, particularly Gentiles, soon wanted to know what the difference was between a Jew and a Christian.

When people try to put their belief into words we call this a **'creed'**. The word 'creed' simply means 'belief'. Some creeds are quite long and complicated and some are very short and easy to remember. The word 'creed' comes from the Latin word 'credo' which means 'I believe'.

The first Christian Creed was probably simply the words 'Jesus is Lord'. It seems that this was what people said when they were baptized. This would have been especially appropriate in the Roman world because the Romans said 'Caesar is Lord' when they sacrificed or burned **incense** in front of a statue of Caesar.

'JESUS IS LORD'

At first there was confusion about Christian belief, and people thought Christians were just another kind of Jewish believer. There were no problems, because the Jews were protected by Roman law. As soon as Christians were seen as different, though, they began to be persecuted because they refused to say 'Caesar is Lord'. Instead they said 'Jesus is Lord'. Although they argued that this made no difference to their loyalty to Caesar, no-one believed them – anyone who would not say 'Caesar is Lord' and burn incense in front of the statue of the Emperor was thought of as a traitor and an enemy of Rome.

It was the first Christian Creed 'Jesus is Lord' which showed how different Christians were from the rest of the people of the Roman Empire. It also showed how different they were from Jews. No Jew could say that anyone was Lord except God. 'The Lord' (Greek 'kurios') was how Jews spoke of God. To them it was **blasphemy** to think of anyone else as 'Lord'. So it was this short creed 'Jesus is Lord' which divided the Christians from the Jewish religion. It also helped Christians begin to work out their own belief that there was only one God, but that Jesus was equal with God and identical to God.

NOTES/DATABASE

Use the glossary to look up the meanings of the following words. Then use the definitions to make your own notes or suitable entries on your database.

Believer	Incense
Creed	Blasphemy

The Roman Emperors, who were called 'Caesar', believed that they were gods. They made the people of the Roman Empire treat them as gods and burn incense in front of their statues saying 'Caesar is Lord'. This showed that the people accepted that the Emperor had complete control over their lives. The Jews were the only people in the Roman Empire who were allowed to refuse to do this because of their belief in one God.

B Statue of Caesar

ACTIVITIES

1 **Quick quiz**

  a When did the first disciples begin to tell other people about Jesus?

  b Why were the believers respected at first?

  c What happened when they began to be persecuted?

  d Where was the name 'Christians' first used?

  e Why do you think this name stuck?

  f Who was one of the first people to become a believer who was not a Jew?

  g Where was the Ethiopian official when he became a believer?

  h Who wanted to know what the difference was between Jews and Christians?

  i What does the word 'creed' mean?

  j What do we think was the first Christian Creed?

  k What did the Romans say about Caesar?

  l Why was it that Jews did not have to say 'Caesar is Lord'?

  m Why did people in the Roman Empire begin to persecute the Christians?

  n How did the words 'Jesus is Lord' show that Christians were different from both Jews and Romans?

  o What did this creed help the Christians to work out about their own belief?

FURTHER ACTIVITIES

I BELIEVE!

What people believe is called their 'creed'. It is not necessarily a belief in God. It can be belief in an ideal or set of ideas. It can also be political belief.

Nelson Mandela was put in prison in South Africa in 1963 for his belief in the equality of black and white people. If he had been prepared to accept the government's conditions, he could have been let out many years ago. He was not prepared to do that. He therefore remained a prisoner. His creed is the belief that black and white people should have equal rights.

Martin Luther King had a similar creed. Here is a part of one of his speeches:

"I have a dream, that one day the grandsons of former slaves, and the grandsons of former slave owners will sit down together . . .

"I have a dream that one day my four little children will be judged, not by the colour of their skin, but by the quality of their lives."

C Martin Luther King

1 What do you believe?

Ask at least six other people the following questions. Try to make sure they are from different age groups:

a Do you believe that men and women should do the same jobs and be paid the same wage?

b Do you think that people of all different races should be treated equally wherever they live in the world?

c Do you believe that health care should be provided free of charge?

d Do you believe that richer countries like Britain and America should help people in poorer countries?

e Do you believe in God?

From the answers to these questions try to write a creed for each of these people. When you have finished, ask each of these people whether it is a fair summary of what they believe.

Now try doing the same thing for yourself. Ask yourself each of the above questions, and then write down your own creed. You may find that you need to add some extra questions to help you work out exactly what your creed is.

SIGNS AND SYMBOLS

2 a What do you think it would be like without signs and symbols? Write down how you think your journey to school would be different if we did not have signs and symbols.

b Quite a lot of things which we buy have symbols on them. These symbols are there to help us. Look inside a piece of clothing for a washing label. Now copy the symbols into your book. Write in words what each symbol tells you.

c Here are some symbols of a different kind! Find out how many people in your class understand the meaning of these symbols.

D A protest march

Even if we can't use these symbols, we all recognize that to some people at least they have meaning, and can be interpreted as sounds.

d Here are some Christian symbols.

Christians recognize these symbols immediately. Find out what each of these symbols means. Each of them has, at some time, been used as a secret symbol, or password, to help Christians to recognize who is a friend.

e Design your own new-style symbol of Christianity.

What kind of people refused to give in to Caesar?

They were people who knew that they did not have to carry the burden of sin around with them. They knew that God had forgiven them for everything they had ever done wrong.

3 Status wasn't important!

a Look up what Paul says in Galatians 3:28. Now write a modern version of this verse in your own words.

b Copy and complete the following chart.

Reference	Person	Occupation
Mark 1:16		
Mark 2:13f		
John 3:1		
Acts 8:28		
Acts 10:1		
Acts 16:14		
Philemon 16		
Acts 16:29		

4 Paul says that Christians have got to stay in training, just like athletes.

Read carefully 1 Corinthians 9:24–27. Why do you think Paul used this picture of what Christians should be like?

5 **Discuss**

Why were the early Christians so brave? How did they stand up for their beliefs? How could they say 'Jesus is Lord' when they were likely to die or be imprisoned for it?

By the second century, the Christians wanted to construct a more accurate statement of what they believed. It was still called a creed, or list of beliefs. There were several attempts at writing a creed before a version was finally accepted by all the Christians.

It is called the Apostles' Creed because it is based on the teachings of the first Apostles. In fact, there is an old story which says that it was actually written by the Apostles. However, it dates from rather later than the time when there would have been any of the original Apostles still alive.

It was very important for the Church to work out what the beliefs of Christianity actually were. As time went on, Christianity became more and more popular. Many more people wanted to join the Church, even though there was danger of persecution. The Creed was used at baptisms, when a person became a full member of the Christian Church. To make sure that the person being baptized really understood what they were doing, they were asked to recite the Creed. They were also expected to agree with everything it said. As soon as someone was baptized, they were a Christian. The moment of baptism was the exact moment when they became Christians. It was also the moment when the very real danger of persecution began. These brave Christians needed to be very sure of what they believed. It was difficult to be a Christian, and it was difficult for them to stand up for their beliefs when they knew it was illegal and they could be punished.

After 311 CE the danger of persecution was over. Constantine had become the new Roman **Emperor**. His mother was a Christian. She was called Helen, and was the daughter of the governor of Britain. Constantine had never expected to be the Emperor. He was a Roman soldier who had fought many battles. Having seen so much death on the battlefield, he was unlikely to believe that he was a god. This meant that Christians were no longer called traitors for refusing to believe that the Emperor was a god.

In 313 CE Constantine passed a law called the **Edict of Milan**. This said that people could be Christians. For the first time it was within the law to be a Christian.

Soon many people began to become Christians without really believing in Jesus. It was rather fashionable to be a Christian. Often the most important jobs would go to Christians. There were public discussions about what Christian belief was all about.

A Ancient baptismal font

B The Arch of the Emperor Constantine, Rome

Constantine called a great council of the leaders of the Church at a place called Nicea. This decided to accept a list of what Christians believe which is called the **Nicene Creed**. This is still used in the Church today, and remains almost identical to the version accepted by Constantine and his Church leaders.

The Nicene Creed

*We believe in one God
the Father the Almighty
maker of heaven and earth,
of all that is,
seen and unseen.*

*We believe in one Lord,
 Jesus Christ,
the only Son of God,
eternally begotten of the Father,
God from God, Light from Light,
true God from true God,
begotten, not made.
For us men and for our salvation
he came down from heaven;
by the power of the Holy Spirit
he became incarnate of the
 Virgin Mary,
and was made Man.
For our sake he was crucified
 under Pontius Pilate;
he suffered death and was buried.
On the third day he rose again
in accordance with the Scriptures;
he ascended into heaven
and is seated at the right hand
 of the Father,
He will come again in glory
to judge the living and the dead,
and his kingdom will have no end.*

*We believe in the Holy Spirit,
the Lord, the Giver of Life, who
 proceeds from the Father and
 the Son.
With the Father and the Son he is
 worshipped and glorified,
He has spoken through the
 prophets.*

*We believe in one holy, catholic and
 Apostolic Church.
We acknowledge one baptism for
 the forgiveness of sins.
We look for the resurrection of the
 dead,
and the life of the world to come.
Amen.*

NOTES/DATABASE

Use the glossary to look up the meanings of the following words. Then use the definitions to make your own notes or suitable entries on your database.

Emperor   Nicene Creed

Edict of Milan

C A chapel in the catacomb of San Sebastiano, Via Appia, Rome

ACTIVITIES

1 **Quick quiz**

a When did the Church start to construct a more accurate statement of what it believed?

b What is a statement of belief called?

c What was the name given to the statement of belief which was accepted by all Christians?

d Why do we think that the original Apostles did not write the Apostles' Creed?

e Why was it surprising that many more people wanted to join the Church?

f On which occasion was the Creed often used?

g What was the significance of baptism?

h Why did baptism put people in danger?

i When was the danger of persecution ended in the Roman Empire?

j Why was persecution no longer a danger?

k Who was Constantine's mother?

l Why did it become fashionable to become a Christian?

m Who called together a great council of the church?

n Where did this council take place?

o What was the result of the council?

p Why do you think the words of the two Creeds are still almost identical to when they were first written?

q Do you think creeds are necessary? Write down some reasons for your answer.

FURTHER ACTIVITIES

BELIEFS AND BAPTISMS

The Creeds are divided into three parts:

a Belief about God.

b Belief about Jesus.

c Other Christian beliefs.

1 Use the Nicene Creed on the previous page to help you to copy and complete the chart.

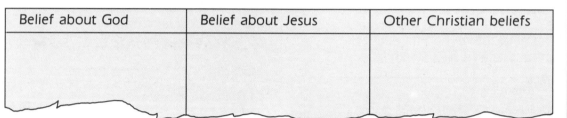

Belief about God	Belief about Jesus	Other Christian beliefs

2 Use a prayer book to find the words of the Apostles' Creed.

By the beginning of the third century, people who wanted to be baptized had to answer questions about what they believed in front of the whole church. Later on, instead of the questions, they had to recite a Creed. After baptism, new Christians were allowed to take part in Holy Communion. This is the service in which Christians receive bread and wine to help them to remember what Jesus did for them by coming to Earth.

D Infant baptism in the Anglican church

E Baptism by immersion in a Baptist Church

The Baptism: Questions and answers in the Church of England

A Do you believe and trust in God the Father?
I believe and trust in God the Father who made me and all the world.

Do you believe and trust in Jesus Christ, His only Son?
I believe and trust in Jesus Christ, who redeemed mankind.

Do you believe and trust in the Holy Spirit?
I believe and trust in the Holy Spirit, who gives life to the people of God.

Parents who want their babies baptized are taught about the Christian faith before the baptism takes place.

The second part of the baptism is when Anglican/Catholic young people can say for themselves what they believe.

When Anglican young people have been baptized and confirmed they can receive Holy Communion.

3 Compare what happened in the Early Church with what happens in the Anglican Church today.

Baptists

In the Baptist Church, as well as Pentecostal, Brethren and House Churches, only adults are baptized. They all have to 'give a testimony' at their baptism. This means that they have to make a short speech about their own personal Christian belief, and why they have become believers in Jesus.

4 a Use the three questions in Box A and write new answers to them in your own words. The answers which are given in the baptism service may help you, but try to write down your own ideas.

b Use your answers to question (a) to help you construct the kind of speech a Baptist might make at a baptism.

When Christianity became legal, Christians were no longer persecuted.

Many people became Christians who did not really believe in Jesus. Later on, Christianity became the only legal religion in the Roman Empire. Everyone had to be a Christian.

CONSTANTINE'S STORY

5 a What did Constantine do before he became emperor?

b Why do you think he might have been in favour of Christianity?

c Explain what Constantine saw in the sky before the battle.

d What did he think this meant?

e What law did Constantine make which helped the Christians?

6 **Discuss**

Do you think that it is right that everyone should have to belong to one religion?

7 **Drama**

The story of Constantine is an exciting one, and worth acting. Write a script to present the story as a play, or make an audio tape with different voices.

8 **Something to think about**

Many of the people who became Christians in the time of Constantine did not believe in Jesus. They didn't want to live the way Jesus suggested.

Some people got fed up with the lack of true belief, and left Rome to become monks. One of these was St Benedict of Nursia. Find out how he began the Benedictine Order of Monks.

The capital of the **Roman Empire** had always been Rome. Constantine decided to create a new capital city right in the centre of the Roman Empire. The place he selected was in the country we now call Turkey, and the city was called Byzantium. When Constantine rebuilt it in 330 CE he changed its name to 'Constantinopolis' (we used to call it Constantinople) which means 'Constantine's city'. In the twentieth century, this was changed to Istanbul.

In many ways, this new Christian city which Constantine had built was in an ideal spot. It was at the point where Europe and Asia meet, and even now it remains a natural crossroads of trade and culture (see map).

It was very important to Constantine that this should be an entirely Christian city. The centre of it was the Church of the Holy Wisdom. No image of the old Roman or Greek gods was allowed to be put anywhere in the city. The **Bishop** of the city where the Emperor lived was an important man. As the adviser to the Emperor, he began to be the equal of the Bishop of Rome who ruled the Church in the West. Soon the **Patriarch** of Constantinople was the leader of the Church in the Eastern part of the Mediterranean.

In those days communications were not very good. It took a long time for the people in the Eastern Church to find out what the people in the Western Church were doing. Gradually, different customs and beliefs grew up. These included the different ways in which they celebrated **Holy Communion** (the service at which Christians eat bread and drink wine to help them to remember why Jesus came to earth and why he died). They also disagreed about whether priests should be allowed to be married, about who the real leader of the Church was, and about the exact words in the **Nicene Creed**.

The Great Schism (this means 'big split') came in 1053 when the **Pope** (the

A Greek Orthodox priest

Bishop of Rome) and the Patriarch of Constantinople disagreed about the way the Church should be governed.

From then onwards, the Church in the Eastern part of the Mediterranean has been separated from the Western Church. The leader of the Western Church was the Pope, and he is still the leader of the Roman Catholic Church. The leader of the Eastern Church is the Patriarch of Constantinople.

The Eastern Church became known as the **Orthodox** Church. The word 'orthodox' means 'correct belief'. There are fifteen separate branches of the Orthodox Church in the world today,

chiefly in Eastern Mediterranean countries, as well as in Russia. Each Church is ruled by a Patriarch. The Patriarch of Constantinople is regarded as a sort of honorary leader by each of the Churches.

Christianity was taken to Russia in 888 CE by St Basil. The main cathedral church in Moscow is named after him. There are 70 million baptized Orthodox Christians in Russia today. About 45 million of these are regular, practising members. Despite the hardships for more than 70 years after the Russian Revolution in 1917, when Christianity was actively discouraged by the USSR, nearly 25 per cent of the Russian population continue to be active members of the Russian Orthodox Church. There are a further 12 million Christians of other denominations.

The Greek Orthodox Church remains one of the strongest of the Orthodox Churches. All over the world there are communities of people who have fled from their native Greece or from other Orthodox countries who still maintain their own national traditions and customs through the Orthodox Church.

B St Basil's Cathedral, Moscow

C The Church of St Sophia, Istanbul

ACTIVITIES

1 **Quick quiz**

a Where did Constantine choose to build his new city?

b What other names has Constantinople had?

c Why do you think Constantine chose this particular spot to build the city?

d How did Constantine try to make sure it was a Christian city?

e Why was the Bishop of Constantinople important?

f What is the leader of the Eastern Church called today?

g What different customs began to grow up?

h What does the name 'Orthodox' mean?

i What does the 'Great Schism' mean?

j How many separate branches of the Orthodox Church are there?

k Why is it surprising that Christianity is so strong in Russia?

l What is the name of another very strong branch of the Orthodox Church?

NOTES/DATABASE

Use the glossary to look up the meanings of the following words. Then use the definitions to make your own notes or suitable entries on your database.

Roman Empire   Nicene Creed

Bishop   Pope

Patriarch   Orthodox

Holy Communion

2 a What is the name of the sea to the north of Constantinople?

b What is the name of the sea to the south of Constantinople?

c Why do you think Constantine chose to build a city on the edge of Bosphorus?

d Which continent was Constantinople in?

e Do you think it was difficult to get to
(i) Asia Minor,
(ii) Russia?

f What geographical reasons can you think of for Constantine choosing to build his new capital city on the site of Byzantium?

3 **Something to think about**

How similar are the reasons for Istanbul's growth to the reasons for which Constantine first chose it as his capital city?

Christians and Muslims now live side by side in Istanbul. It is a crossroads of the two different cultures.

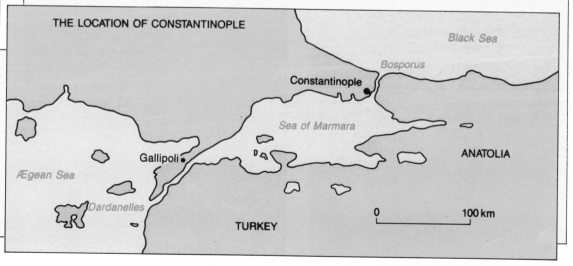

THE LOCATION OF CONSTANTINOPLE

Black Sea

Bosporus

Constantinople

Sea of Marmara

Gallipoli

Ægean Sea

ANATOLIA

Dardanelles

0   100 km

TURKEY

FURTHER ACTIVITIES

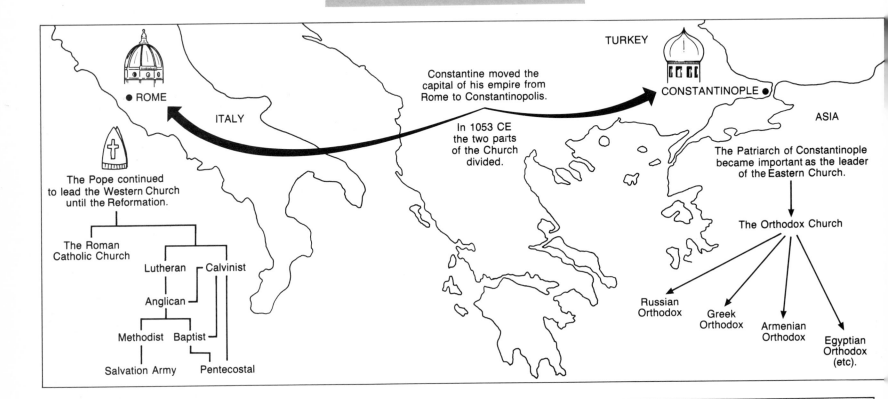

ROME

ITALY

The Pope continued to lead the Western Church until the Reformation.

The Roman Catholic Church — Lutheran — Calvinist — Anglican — Methodist — Baptist — Salvation Army — Pentecostal

Constantine moved the capital of his empire from Rome to Constantinopolis.

In 1053 CE the two parts of the Church divided.

TURKEY

CONSTANTINOPLE

ASIA

The Patriarch of Constantinople became important as the leader of the Eastern Church.

The Orthodox Church — Russian Orthodox, Greek Orthodox, Armenian Orthodox, Egyptian Orthodox (etc).

1 Use reference books to find out the main reasons for the division of the Church in 1053.

Now produce an in-depth news report about what happened. Brief people to represent Eastern and Western viewpoints. Make sure that the interviewers sum up the arguments clearly.

2 **Discuss**

a Do you think that Christians today would want to disagree for the same reasons as they did in 1053?

b What kind of things are Christians divided over now?

DIFFERENCES BETWEEN ORTHODOX AND CATHOLIC CHURCHES

Differences	Orthodox	Catholic
Language	Greek or local language.	Latin until 1965, now local language as well.
Baptism	Babies baptized naked and dipped right under water.	Water sprinked on adults and babies.
Holy Communion	Bread dipped in wine given at baptism.	First Holy Communion at age seven. Bread and wine kept separate. For many centuries only priests had wine.
Priests	Must be married.	May not be married.
Bishops	Chosen from deacons, must not be married.	Chosen from priests.
Leader	Patriarch of Constantinople.	Bishop of Rome (The Pope).

3 a What language would you expect the service to be in if you attended a Greek Orthodox Church?

b In what ways would an Orthodox baptism differ from one in the Catholic Church (or the Church of England)?

c What is the leader of the Orthodox Church called?

d What difference is there in the way bishops are chosen in the Orthodox and Catholic Churches?

e What important difference in belief is there between the Catholic and Orthodox Church?

4 There are many Orthodox Christians in the following countries:

Egypt	USSR
Greece	Syria
Israel	Turkey
Lebanon	Yugoslavia
Romania	

a Copy the map into your book.

b Find each of these countries on the map. Then colour the countries where many of the people are Orthodox Christians. Colour in the key too.

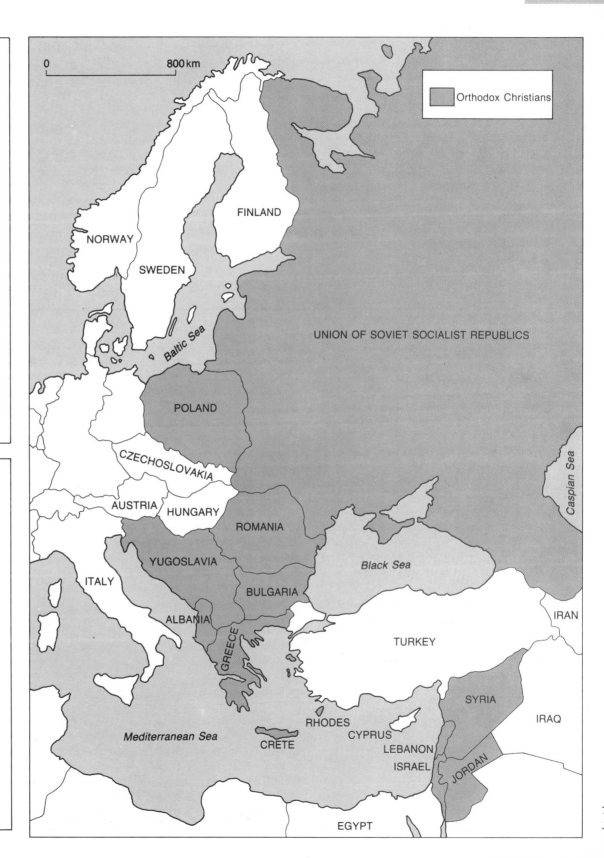

Orthodox Christians

During the twentieth century there have been many occasions when people have had to move from their own countries. Whenever this has happened, people have tried to re-establish the kind of religious practices they were used to in their own countries. Many Orthodox Christians have been forced to leave Eastern Europe, and have found new homes in other countries.

There are a number of groups of Orthodox Christians in Britain. One of these communities is the Church of St Lazarus near Birmingham.

The Church is not only a religious centre for the Yugoslavian community who worship there, but also a social centre. Through the Church, they keep alive the language and traditions of their homeland.

As in any other Orthodox Church, the church services are at the centre of the life of the Christians who meet there. The priest is not only the person who leads the worship, but is also a family friend and adviser, as well as a link with Yugoslavian life and culture.

Many of the services are colourful festivals. The church itself is highly coloured with many beautiful paintings about the life of Jesus painted as **frescos** on the walls.

There are many **ikons** which the people kiss as they enter the church. Most Orthodox families will also have ikons in their own homes. Families have their own special saint, and ikons are often associated with this saint. When families celebrate their own saint's days, the priest often comes to their house to bless the ikon as well as special food which has been prepared for the festival. He will share in a special meal with the family. The bread which is blessed at this ceremony is called **Slava bread**. It has the initials of Christ imprinted on the top.

Orthodox families away from their native lands have found that the Church helps them to keep a sense of identity, and of belonging to their own homeland.

The same is true in war-torn countries where no-one knows what horrors tomorrow will bring. The Orthodox Church in the Lebanon has helped many people there to make sense of life in a world where everyone seems to be killing one another.

A Lebanese Orthodox **delegate** to the World Council of Churches once told this story:

"When the war and the bombing were at their worst in Beirut, the Christians who worshipped together needed each other most. They never stopped telling people about Jesus. Despite the difficulties, they continued to run their Sunday School. A small girl of eight years old began to attend the Sunday School. The leaders found out that she was a Muslim, so they went to her father and told him that she had been coming to the Christian Church. He said that coming pleased the child, and that she might continue to come to Sunday School.

A An English Orthodox church

B Yugoslavian dancers

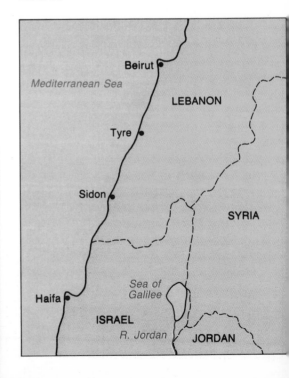

C A church in Beirut

"After some months, it was Easter, and the children talked about the Resurrection of Jesus. The child said, 'I don't know Jesus very well yet, but I think that if I did, we should be good friends,' Later that day, the planes flew again over Beirut, and the area was bombed. Amongst the rubble they found a small arm, still clutching a doll. It was all that remained of the child. Her death, grieved by both Christians and Muslims, gave meaning to the **Resurrection**, and helped to unite both Christians and Muslims in that war-torn city."

Christians and everyone else in Lebanon have to live with incidents like this, and to come to terms with the grief and the sadness. The Orthodox Church, like other Christian Churches all over the world, helps to make sense of life in the middle of the agony of war.

NOTES/DATABASE

Use the glossary to look up the meanings of the following words. Then use the definitions to make your own notes or suitable entries on your database.

Fresco   Delegate

Ikon   Resurrection

Slava bread

ACTIVITIES

1 Quick quiz

a Why do you think that people who have had to leave their native countries try to re-establish their religious practices in their new home?

b In what ways does the church of St Lazarus in Birmingham help the Yugoslavian people who worship there?

c What kind of things does the priest do?

d What are frescos?

e What is an ikon?

f How do families celebrate their saint's day?

g What is on the top of the Slava bread?

2 Look in a cook book!

Try your local library for a recipe for Slava bread, and then make a list of the ingredients. Draw a design for the initials of Christ (this is usually IHS – these are the initials for the Greek words for 'Jesus son of God, our Saviour') to print on the top of Slava bread.

You might be able to make this either at home, and bring it to school for everyone to share, or in your Food Studies lessons.

Plan a menu for a Yugoslavian festival meal, and design some

D Slava bread

menu cards for it. These could be done on the computer if you have a suitable program.

3 Being a Christian when there is a war on.

a Collect information about the Lebanon. It is often in the news. Try and work out why there are wars there.

b The Church Missionary Society has a video about Lebanon called 'Where is Jesus?'. Try to borrow a copy of this to watch.

c Imagine you are one of the Christian children living in the refugee camps. Use the information you have collected as well as the information on this page to help you write a diary for a few days in your life. Use the information about the Orthodox Church in Units 17 and 18 to help you explain what the church service was like which you, as a refugee, attended on Sunday.

FURTHER ACTIVITIES

1 How observant are you?

   a Describe the way the priest is dressed in picture E.

   b How is the priest dressed in picture F?

F Priest swinging an incense burner in an Orthodox church

E Orthodox priest in street clothes

G Orthodox communion service

   c Do you think that the people kneel, sit or stand during the service? Write down some reasons for your answer.

   d How do you think that the people receive the bread and wine at Holy Communion?

SAINTS AND IKONS

2 The Orthodox churches often have beautiful paintings on wood.

They are usually of Jesus or the saints. Sometimes they tell a story from the life of Jesus. They are called ikons. Many Orthodox homes have an ikon of their patron saint.

   a Look carefully at the picture of the ikon. Now design your own ikon.

If you were born on or near a particular saint's day, then that saint would be your patron saint.

   b Find out the nearest saint's day to your birthday. Then look up that saint in a dictionary of saints or of the Church to discover the reason that this person was so famous.

H Ikon of a saint

I Ikon of a biblical scene

RUSSIAN RELIGIONS

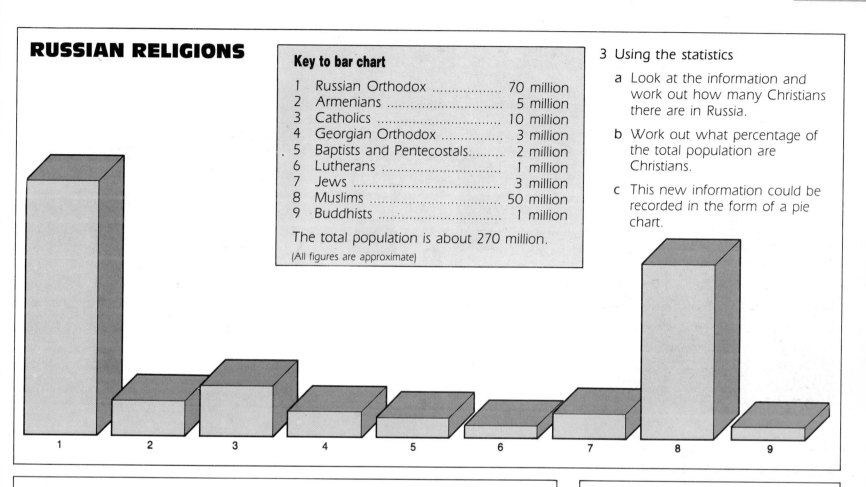

Key to bar chart

1	Russian Orthodox	70 million
2	Armenians	5 million
3	Catholics	10 million
4	Georgian Orthodox	3 million
5	Baptists and Pentecostals	2 million
6	Lutherans	1 million
7	Jews	3 million
8	Muslims	50 million
9	Buddhists	1 million

The total population is about 270 million.

(All figures are approximate)

3 Using the statistics

a Look at the information and work out how many Christians there are in Russia.

b Work out what percentage of the total population are Christians.

c This new information could be recorded in the form of a pie chart.

Religion in Russia

Before 'Glasnost', the Russian word for allowing more freedom, Christian children had a very difficult time at school.

They were not given the same opportunities as other children. Often they were unable to go to university, or even to get a job. Sometimes they were taken away from their parents.

This is what a teacher wrote about trying to find out which of the children were Christians:

"We used to ask the children to draw a picture of God. The children with unbelieving parents answered, "What a silly question! There is no God." But the children of believing parents drew an old man with a beard. Another method was to play a game where we would ask the children to come to the front and sing a song. Quite often the children of believing parents would sing a Sunday School chorus, and so would give their parents away without knowing."

4 a What were the methods used to find out which children were from homes where they believed in God?

b Do you think that parents should be able to choose what they teach their own children?

c Do you think that the government should be allowed to say what children are taught by their parents?

d **Discuss**

(i) Do you think that children are likely to choose to become Christians in the circumstances described here?

(ii) Why do you think that the Russian Church is so strong?

For several centuries after the Eastern Church and the Western Church became divided, the one Church in the West was known as the Catholic Church.

LATIN: THE LANGUAGE OF EDUCATION

Most educated people in the West spoke Latin, and so the language of the Church was Latin.

Official documents were also written in Latin, so quite often high officials were also priests or clergy, because they spoke Latin.

A Aylesford Priory, Kent

The laity – all the ordinary people.

Priests look after the laity who worship in the parish churches.

Bishops look after a diocese – or an area which has about 200 parishes.

A few bishops are chief bishops or "Archbishops."

Cardinals are important bishops who help the Pope govern the Church. They choose the new Pope.

The Pope is the leader of the Roman Catholic Church.

MONKS AND MONASTERIES

Many clergy were also **monks**. The monks lived in monasteries. As well as praying and copying the Bible, the monks were teachers. They also looked after the sick, helped the poor, and provided lodgings for travellers and pilgrims.

During the Middle Ages, the church was the centre of life. Everyone lived in a **parish** and was a Christian.

THE WIND OF CHANGE

The Church was very powerful until the time we call the **Reformation**, which happened in the sixteenth century. The invention of printing, and therefore cheaper printed Bibles being available, made many people question what the Church said. Other Churches began to be formed all over Europe, which used the local languages of the people rather than Latin.

THE ROMAN CATHOLIC CHURCH NOW

The Roman Catholic Church is still the biggest Christian Church. The word 'catholic' means 'universal'. There are Catholic Churches all over the world.

Until 1965, the Roman Catholic Church continued to use Latin in the services. This was so that the services would be the same wherever you went in the world. Although Latin is still used

B St Peter's, Rome

sometimes, most services are now in local languages. By 1582 there was a Catholic version of the Bible in English. (Tyndale's unofficial version was published in 1525, and there were English Bibles in all English Churches by 1539.)

BELIEF

Roman Catholic Christians have similar beliefs to all other Christians. They accept the Creeds as the basis for their belief.

SOME SPECIAL THINGS WHICH CATHOLICS BELIEVE

Roman Catholic Christians also have some extra beliefs which are not shared by all non-Catholic Christians. (Christians who are not Catholic are often described as 'Protestants'.)

C The Pope giving the blessing from the Vatican

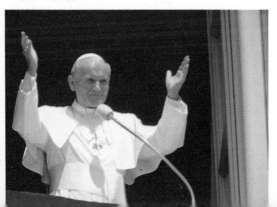

LEADERSHIP

All the ordinary Catholic believers are called laity. The laity usually worship at a church which is looked after by a parish priest. Only priests are allowed to bless the bread and wine for the Mass and to assure people that God has forgiven their sins. (Look at the Table of Sacraments on the next page to help explain the Mass and penance.)

Some priests become bishops. There are usually about 200 parishes in a **diocese**, which is the area looked after by a bishop.

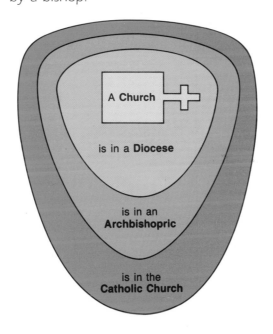

A Church

is in a **Diocese**

is in an **Archbishopric**

is in the **Catholic Church**

D Since the Middle Ages the people of Switzerland have provided the Pope's bodyguard

There are also some chief bishops who are called archbishops, and some of these are also **cardinals**. The cardinals have the job of electing the **Pope** who is the leader of the whole church.

MARY

Roman Catholics have a special place for Mary, the Mother of Jesus. Many churches are dedicated to her, and many homes have statues of Mary.

THE ROSARY

Many Roman Catholics use a **rosary** to help them to pray. Look at the labelled picture of the Rosary.

small beads: here you say the Hail Mary

The linking bead is often a reminder about some Holy Place like Lourdes.

large beads: here you say the Lord's Prayer

A crucifix —you say the Creed

Hail Mary full of grace, the Lord is with thee.

Blessed art thou amongst women and blessed is the fruit of thy womb Jesus.

Holy Mary, Mother of God, pray for us sinners now and in the hour of our death. Amen.

THE ROMAN CATHOLIC CHURCH

NOTES/DATABASE

Use the glossary to look up the meanings of the following words. Then use the definitions to make your own notes or suitable entries on your database.

Monk   Shrine   Diocese

Parish   Pope   Cardinal

Reformation   Rosary

ACTIVITIES

1 **Quick quiz**

a What was the name given to the Church in the West?

b What language was used by educated people in the West?

c In the Middle Ages, what kind of things did the monks do to help people?

d Who was a member of the Church in the Middle Ages?

e What difference did the invention of printing make in the sixteenth century?

f What good reason was there for going on having church services in Latin?

g When was the first Roman Catholic version of the English Bible?

h What do Roman Catholics accept as the basis of their beliefs?

i Name two things which only priests can do.

j What is the name for an area looked after by bishop?

k Describe briefly how a rosary is used.

2 Sacraments

Look at the seven pictures below. These are pictures of the seven Sacraments.

Match each picture with the correct name and explanation of what is happening – you will find these in the chart below.

Sacrament	Reason	Sign
Eucharist	Recalling the Last Supper which Jesus had with the disciples on the night before he was crucified.	Bread and wine
Baptism	Becoming a member of the Christian Church. A sign that God is ready to forgive people who are sorry for what they have done wrong.	Water
Confirmation	The second part of baptism, when someone takes for themselves the promises which their parents made for them when they were baptized.	Laying on of hands
Ordination	Giving someone the Church's authority to be a deacon, priest or bishop.	Laying on of hands by a bishop
Marriage	Two people promising before God that they will be faithful to each other for the rest of their lives.	Giving and receiving of a ring
Penance	Showing that someone is sorry for what they have done wrong, and that God is ready to forgive.	The person who is sorry tells the priest what they have done wrong, and the priest assures them that God has already forgiven them
The Sacrament of the Sick	Showing that God can heal people and help them in times of trouble.	anointing with oil

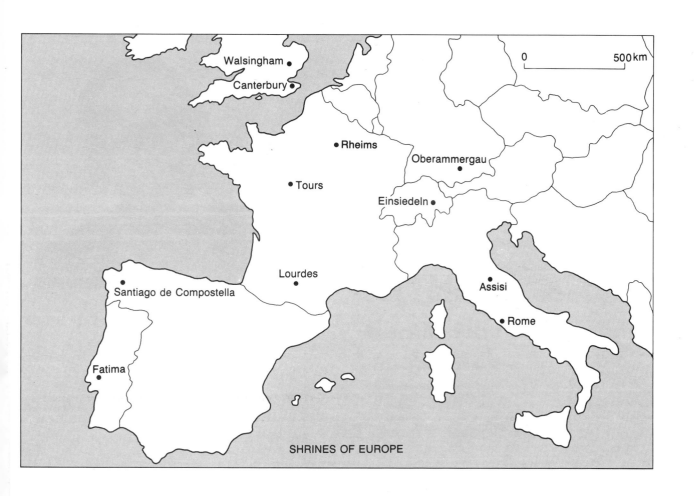

SHRINES OF EUROPE

3 Look at the map of Europe.

You will notice that there are pictures of places of pilgrimage in several countries. People have visited some of these places for hundreds of years.

Find out why each of these is a famous place of pilgrimage. Copy and complete the chart by filling in the country where each **shrine** is, and the reason why people visit that shrine.

Shrine	Country	Reason
Walsingham		
Canterbury		
Lourdes		
Fatima		
Santiago de Compostella		
Rome		
Assisi		
Oberammergau		
Einsiedeln		
Tours		
Rheims		

BEING A CHRISTIAN NOW: OSCAR ROMERO

Throughout his life, Jesus was involved with ordinary people in their own, often difficult circumstances. His message was to everyone, but it has been said he was biased towards the poor. The poor, he said, will be the ones who inherit the Kingdom of God. What does Jesus mean by this?

In recent years, Christians have begun to explore what it means to be like Christ. For some, this has meant standing on the side of the oppressed and the underdog. For others, it has meant taking part in political struggles to help people.

Some Christians argue that Jesus' words and actions constantly brought him into conflict with the political authorities of his day. Therefore, if Christians follow his teaching closely, they too will sometimes be in conflict with the political authorities.

Here is a letter written by a Roman Catholic archbishop named Oscar Romero who was the Archbishop of El Salvador in Central America. He believed that it was right to speak out against injustice wherever he saw it.

WANTED
This man is dangerous!
PETER
Bishop of Rome

WANTED

OSCAR ROMERO
Archbishop of El Salvador

THIS MAN IS DANGEROUS

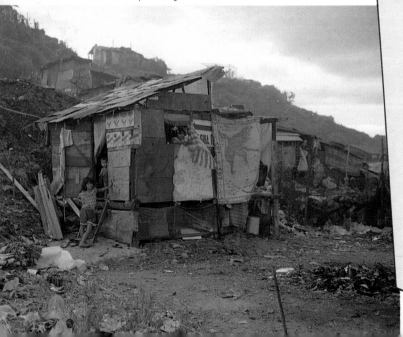

A Third World poverty

Dear Mr President,

A recent news item in the press has concerned me very much. According to the article, your administration is studying the possibility of backing the present government junta and giving it economic and military aid. Because you are a Christian and have said that you want to defend human rights, I take the liberty to express my pastoral point of view on this matter, and of making a specific request.

I am deeply disturbed over the news that the US government is studying a way to accelerate El Salvador's arms race by sending military teams and advisers . . . this . . . will intensify the injustice and repression of the common people who are organized to struggle for respect of their most basic human rights. Since I am Salvadorian and Archbishop of the San Salvador diocese I have the obligation to work for the reign of faith and justice . . . I urge you to prohibit the giving of military assistance . . . to guarantee that your government will not intervene . . .

I hope your religious sentiments and your sensitivity for the defence of human rights will move you to accept my request, and thereby avoid greater bloodshed in our long-suffering country.

Sincerely,
Oscar Romero
Archbishop
Feb 17 1980

One month later, Oscar Romero was dead, murdered while saying Mass in his own cathedral.

ACTIVITIES

1 Quick quiz

a Towards which group of people was Jesus biased?

b What kind of things have Christians begun to get involved with as they have explored what it means to be like Christ?

c How did Jesus get into trouble with the political authorities?

d Who was Oscar Romero?

e What did Oscar Romero believe it was right to do?

f Why did Archbishop Romero write to the President of the USA?

g What did he ask the President to do?

h What did Romero think would avoid more bloodshed in El Salvador?

i How did the Archbishop die?

2 Find out

Copy and complete the following chart with the names of organizations which help people in Column A, and the type of work that they do in Column B. Some examples have been done for you.

A	B
Christian Aid	Famine relief
Oxfam	
Save the Children Fund	

3 Plan an advertising campaign

Choose **one** of the organizations in your list, and try to find out as much as you can about the work it does. You might like to write to the organization you have chosen for some extra information.

NOW

Either

a Prepare a talk to give to the whole class about this organization,

or

b In groups, design an advertising campaign for this charity. You will need to know exactly what the aims of the charity are, as well as ways in which you can help ordinary people to understand more about its work.

If you have a computer, use a desktop publishing program to design posters and a brochure for the charity. Use a spreadsheet program to help you to work out the cost of your advertising campaign.

It might also be possible to record an 'appeal' for your charity on audio tape, which could be played in Assembly.

The charity you have chosen will certainly be interested in your work. Do send them details, as well as asking for their help.

FURTHER ACTIVITIES

1 Discuss

Why do you think someone might want to spend their life serving God by being a priest?

2 A visit to a Roman Catholic church

You might like to invite your local Catholic priest to visit you, or perhaps you could visit the local Catholic church.

If you visit the church you might:

a Draw a plan of the church.

b Find out if there are any other important rooms attached to the church.

c Notice the smell . . . and find out what it is!

d Find out who the church is 'dedicated' to, and what services they have on Sundays and weekdays.

e Look for the altar, the font, the reserved sacrament, the penance box, the pulpit.

f Ask to see the vestments, and find out about their different colours.

An invitation

Fulston Manor School, Sittingbourne.

Dear Father.................
3c would like to find out more about what a priest does. We know that he takes church services, but would like to discover what else he does.
We would be very grateful if you could come along and talk to us about your job. We would also like to know why you decided to be a priest.
  Yours Sincerely
  3c.

B Catholic priest chatting to children

C Interior of a Catholic church

3 Follow up

a After your research, write your own version of the diary of a parish priest, including a Sunday and the rest of the week.

b Design your own church noticeboard. Include all the events and services which you think should take place in the church each week.

ST MARY'S CHURCH

Priest...

Sunday Masses...

Confessions...

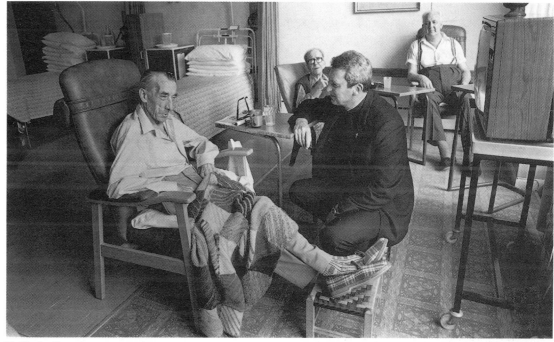

E Catholic priest at work

D Exterior of a Catholic church

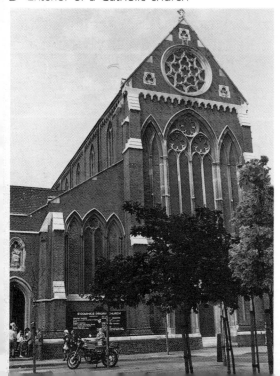

SUNDAY

8 a.m. Mass (celebrate)
9 a.m. Mass (Preach)
11 a.m. Mass (Preach)
5.30 p.m. Benediction

MONDAY

TUESDAY

Assembly - St. Peter's School 9 a.m.
Visit Mrs Jones 10.30 a.m.

WEDNESDAY

THURSDAY

FRIDAY

Lunch with Bishop 1 p.m.

SATURDAY

Confessions 5.30 p.m. →

In most towns you will find a variety of different churches. Nearly every village in England has a parish church. These are usually **Anglican** churches, or 'Church of England'.

There are Anglican churches in many countries of the world. Although each of the national churches is independent, with its own organization and bishops and other leaders, they all look on the Archbishop of Canterbury as their leader.

Some of these churches have different rules from the others. For example, some national churches allow women to be **ordained**, whilst others have not taken that step.

A 1988 Conference of Anglican Bishops, Canterbury

B A woman bishop

Anglican churches in England are often old buildings. Some of them are many centuries old. The ancient architecture is often very beautiful. Here is a picture of one of the oldest churches in the country.

C St Michael's, Amberley

However, some of them are very new and contain more functional features, including special rooms for playgroups and youth clubs, kitchens and toilets.

D A modern church

In England, everyone lives in a parish. They have the right to be married, baptized and buried in their own parish church. Do you know which parish you live in?

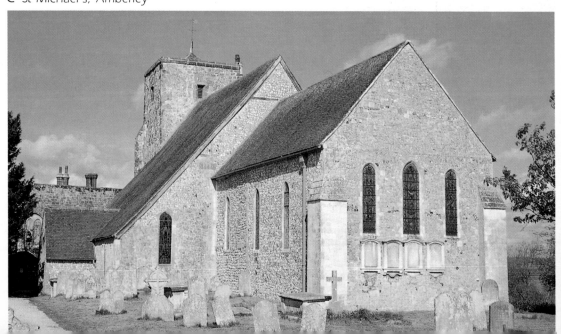

VICARS AND PARISHES

Most parishes have a **vicar**. He is the parish priest or minister for that parish. He organizes the services on Sundays as well as being reponsible for all the weekday activities which are organized from his church. Much of his time is spent visiting. Sometimes he visits sick people, sometimes old people. Often people in the parish want to talk over their problems with someone reliable, and the vicar is often asked to help people with problems.

Sometimes the vicar has a curate to help him. The curate will usually be a younger man who has been ordained. He is an assistant to the vicar, and will one day have a parish of his own.

More often, a vicar has to look after several parishes – sometimes as many as six. Sometimes he may have a parish **deacon** to help. He or she will lead many of the services in the churches, but is not allowed to bless the bread and wine at Holy Communion. Only a priest is allowed to do that. Very often there are also **readers**. These are ordinary people who have been trained to preach and lead services. They have ordinary jobs as well, but help with the church whenever they can.

The main part of the vicar's job, however, is the same as any other Christian, and the same as the job which Jesus originally gave to the first disciples. That is, telling other people about Jesus, and helping them to understand a little more about how God wants people to live their lives.

BISHOPS AND DIOCESES

Every parish is part of a diocese. A bishop is in charge of a diocese. Every diocese has a cathedral, or mother church. Usually there are about two hundred parishes in a diocese. The Diocesan Bishop goes to the parish churches for special events like **confirmations**. For special events when they need a really large church, people from the parishes will go to the cathedral. For example, ordinations (see Sacraments chart, Chapter 19) usually take place in the cathedral. Often, the cathedral provides a central place for celebrations like the annual Canterbury Youth Pilgrimage.

E The Lambeth Conference 1988 procession entering Canterbury Cathedral

F Glastonbury Youth Pilgrimage

ACTIVITIES

1 **Quick quiz**

a What is another name for the Church of England?

b Who do Anglicans in all countries regard as their leader?

c Write down one of the rules of the Church which is not the same in every country.

d Who can be married in church in any parish in this country?

e Who organizes the services in each church?

f What does a curate do?

g What is a parish deacon?

h What kind of things would you expect a reader to do?

i Who is in charge of a diocese?

j What kind of things would you expect a cathedral to be used for?

FURTHER ACTIVITIES

FIND OUT YOUR PARISH AND YOUR DIOCESE

1 Mapwork

Make sure you know the ordnance survey symbols for churches.

Church with a tower **Church with a spire** **Church with no tower or spire**

On a map of your area, find each of the local churches.

Now try to find out which church belongs to each different denomination, and when each church was built.

Display your findings in a chart like the one below.

Name	Address	Denomination	Date
St Michael	High Street	Anglican	1500
St Mary	Park Rd	Roman Catholic	1850
Methodist	High St	Methodist	1880
Baptist Church	High St	Baptist	1935

You will notice that very often there are more Anglican churches in a town than any other kind. This is because the Anglican Church is the 'established Church' in this country. Church leaders attend many national functions. Royal weddings and baptisms take place in Anglican churches, and the Sovereign (the King or the Queen) is the legal head of the Church of England.

At the Reformation, all the churches in England became Anglican churches. For some years it was forbidden to be a member of any other church. Therefore other churches were built later when people became more tolerant.

G Cambridge city centre

2 Find out which diocese your town is in.

Now look up the address of your Diocesan Office in the 'phone book. If you write and ask them, the Diocesan Office may send you a copy of the map of the different parishes in your area. Display the map on the wall and use coloured pins to display which parishes you each live in.

3 A typical Medieval parish church

Here is a plan of a typical Medieval Anglican parish church. Compare it with the plan you drew of the Catholic church. Is there anything that you found in the Catholic church which you cannot find in the Anglican church?

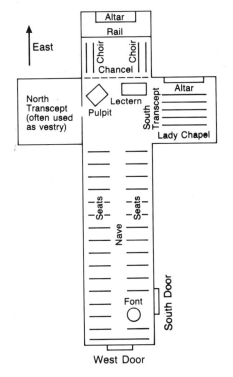

Now answer these questions.

a What shape is the church?

b Where is the altar?

c Why do you think there are often stained-glass windows in a church?

d Can you think of any reason why the font should be near the door?

e Do you think it is a good idea to seat the choir between the congregation and the altar?

4 Design your own church!

ECCLESIASTICAL ARCHITECTS REQUIRED FOR AN EXCITING NEW PROJECT

DESIGN THE CHURCH OF THE TWENTY-FIRST CENTURY.

Your group are the new firm of church architects. You have to design a church for a new housing estate. If you have a CAD system on your computer, you might like to use it to produce your plans.

You will need to decide on

a The number of seats you require in your church.

b The arrangement of seats.

c The type of musical instruments you intend using for services.

d Do you need a choir? Will they need a **vestry**? Does the vicar need an office?

e What weekday activities do you plan to be attached to your church? (It will help to list these, and then work out what the requirements are for each activity.)

f What kind of heating do you think you need to install?

g Car parking arrangements.

h What toilet facilities do you need?

You might find it helpful to discuss these points, and any others which you can think of, with local vicars. Many churches or even your cathedral might be interested in displaying the results of your ideas for a new church design.

When you have designed your church, you will know a great deal about the kind of activities which go on in churches. Imagine that the Reverend Bloggs is the new vicar of your church. Write a letter from him to an old college friend describing some of the exciting things which are happening in his new church.

---

5 What does a vicar do?

Is it really a Sunday-only job?

Look back at Unit 19 where it is suggested that you ask the Roman Catholic parish priest to visit your school and tell you about his work. You might like to invite the Anglican vicar along too. It would be interesting to compare the work of the Catholic priest with that of the Anglican vicar.

6 Some people wear funny clothes!

Here are some of the special clothes which some people wear in church. Make a collage of a scene in a cathedral with a choir, a bishop, priests and servers dressed in these traditional garments.

Find out why there are different colours for different times of the year.

7 Plan a youth service

The Church of England uses a prayer book called the 'Alternative Service Book'. Use the outline for morning prayer and plan (in groups) a special service for teenagers. Include your favourite hymns, and choose prayers which are appropriate. (It might be possible to use this for an Assembly.)

Server Crucifer Server Choristers Deacon Priest Bishop

People are all different, and they like to be able to worship God in different ways. That is one of the reasons why there are so many different churches in towns.

METHODIST CHURCHES

Most towns will have a Methodist church.

These were begun in the eighteenth century by a great preacher called John Wesley. He travelled all over England on horseback. Everywhere he went, people gathered to hear him preach and explain the Bible in ways they could understand.

When Wesley lived, England was very strictly divided into parishes, just as it is now. John Wesley said, "I look upon the whole world as my **parish**." Local vicars often refused to let him preach in their churches because his preaching was so popular. He and his brother liked to write hymns with rousing tunes which people enjoyed singing. They encouraged everyone to want to read their Bibles and to learn more about the way God wanted them to live.

When **vicars** refused to allow Wesley into their churches, he started preaching in the fields and market places. He also found time to write books and **sermons** which were very popular.

Soon so many people were interested in the Wesleyan way of preaching and explaining the Bible that more teachers and preachers encouraged people who learned something to pass it on to someone else, and so he organized people into 'classes'.

Eventually a new Church was formed, called the Wesleyan, or Methodist, Church. In many ways it was, and is, similar to the Church of England. However, Methodists do not believe that their ministers should be called priests.

BAPTIST CHURCHES

Baptist churches are also found in most towns. The important difference between the Baptists and the Anglicans and Roman Catholics is that the Baptists believe it is wrong to **baptize** babies.

Baptism, they believe, is so important that only people who have made up their own minds that they want to be Christians for the rest of their lives should be baptized. Then, after they have learned about the Christian faith, they should be baptized by full **immersion**. That means they should be ducked right under the water as a sign that they have stopped going their own way in life, but want to go God's way instead.

THE SALVATION ARMY

In the nineteenth century, there was a great deal of poverty and misery, particularly in the big cities like London. William Booth was a remarkable man who wanted to do something about the awful conditions, and at the same time to help poor people to know about God.

JOHN 1703 - Founder of Methodism

WESLEY - 1791 Hymn writer

"I regard the whole world as my parish"

GEORGIA AMERICA 1735–1736 In charge of a mission in America

At Oxford he joined a group called "Methodists"

ADVICE TO JOHN WESLEY
"Preach faith until you have faith. Then when you have faith... ...preach faith!"

MORAVIAN MISSION Fetter Lane
Wesley experienced "conversion"

Wesley began to preach in the open air, travelling everywhere on horseback.

An old foundry near Moorfields was the first Methodist Chapel.

BRISTOL
Bristol became his headquarters.

METHODISM IS NOW SPREAD THROUGHOUT THE WORLD.

He felt that the Church of England was only scratching the surface of trying to help people. In the East End of London, William Booth set up centres where poor people could receive help. Like Wesley, he went out on the street corners where ordinary people could hear the Good News about Jesus. Just as Wesley liked to use rousing hymns which were easy to sing, so did William Booth and the Salvation Army. They brought encouragement and help to many.

It was against this background that the Salvation Army began. It is now at work in almost every area of the world. When there are problems and disasters, the Salvation Army is one of the first organizations to be called in to help. Their commitment to helping people has earned them respect all over the world.

A A Salvation Army band

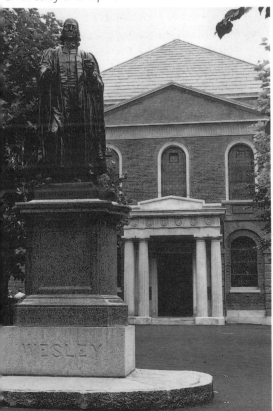

B Wesley's Chapel

OTHER CHURCHES IN YOUR AREA

You may have discovered other churches in your towns. Some of you may have found House Churches, Pentecostal churches, Brethren, Seventh Day Adventists, and many others. Each of them tries, in their own way, to interpret the teachings of Jesus Christ and the message of the Bible.

ACTIVITIES

1 **Quick quiz**

a Why did people like to listen to John Wesley preaching?

b What kind of hymns did the Wesley brothers write?

c Where did Wesley preach?

d Why did Wesley organize people into 'classes'?

e What is the main difference between the Baptist Church and the Church of England?

f Why do Baptists believe that only adults should be baptized?

g What does 'full immersion' mean?

h Why did William Booth want to help people?

i Where did William Booth begin to preach?

j What similarities can you see between William Booth and John Wesley?

k Why do you think that the Salvation Army is so respected all over the world?

NOTES/DATABASE

Use the glossary to look up the meanings of the following words. Then use the definitions to make your own notes or suitable entries on your database.

Parish   Baptize

Vicar   Immersion

Sermon

2 Design a fact sheet

Choose one of the following Churches, and compile a fact sheet about it. There may be one of them in your area. If so, try to visit the building and find out how it is different from the other churches you have visited.

Brethren (the building is usually called a 'Gospel Hall')

Seventh Day Adventist

Pentecostal

If you can, use a computer to prepare the text of your fact sheet. A desktop publishing system is ideal for this purpose.

FURTHER ACTIVITIES

JOHN WESLEY: THE FOUNDER OF METHODISM

1 **Setting out to preach the gospel**

Look up Luke 9:1–6.

a What instructions did Jesus give the disciples when he sent them out to preach?

b Do you think that Jesus would have approved of the way John Wesley went around on horseback preaching everywhere in England?

c What reasons can you think of for so many ordinary people being convinced by the preaching of John Wesley?

2 **If it is possible to arrange it, visit a Methodist church.**

a Draw a plan of the Methodist church. List the similarities and differences between the Methodist church and other churches you have visited.

b Try to arrange an interview with a Methodist minister. If you are able to do this, ask the kind of questions which will help you to build up a picture of what he does each week. Then write a diary of his weekly activities. How similar are these to those of other clergy you have interviewed?

> **Video production team required:**
> For an exciting new video based on the life of John Wesley, the founder of Methodism.

3 Look up John Wesley in an encyclopaedia.

His life story would make an exciting play or video. To produce it, you would need researchers, script writers, actors, directors and possibly a film crew.

If you are able to use a video camera, John Wesley's life would make an interesting film. If possible, use a word processor to write your script – it is easy to update if you want to change something. You might also like to ask someone artistic to design a sleeve for your video.

Finally, your local Methodist church might very well be interested in the project. If you have presented it as a play, there might be a chance to perform it for the Methodist church, or if you have made a video then they might like to have a copy and to come to the premier (the first time it is shown).

C The baptismal pool in a Baptist church

IF YOU BELIEVE WITH ALL YOUR HEART, THEN YOU MAY BE BAPTIZED!

Baptists believe that people should not be baptized unless they have really decided for themselves that they want to follow Jesus.

The first Baptists were a group of people in Zurich who began to rebaptize adults in 1525. At first they were called Anabaptists. The first Baptist church in England began in 1611 at Spitalfields in London. Many of the Roundheads who fought with Cromwell were Baptists, and many of the early settlers in America were also Baptists.

One of the best known British Baptists was John Bunyan, who wrote 'Pilgrim's Progress'. He spent nearly eighteen years in prison for preaching about Baptist beliefs.

Basic beliefs of the Baptists

a The Bible is the only guide to faith and action.

b Only people who are old enough to know what they really believe, and who 'know the Lord Jesus for themselves' may be baptized.

c Baptism should always be by complete immersion. That means going right down under the water. It is a symbol of making a completely new start in life.

d Everyone can have a personal direct relationship with God. They do not need anyone else to act for them or to tell them what to believe.

e Every Baptist church is self-governing, but most are linked to all the others through the Baptist Union.

4 Some questions to answer

a Who were the Anabaptists?

b Where and when did the first Baptist church start in England?

c Which famous Baptist was imprisoned for eighteen years?

d Can you think of any reason why some of the first settlers in America were Baptist?

e In which country were Baptists imprisoned for their faith until recently?

f What do Baptists believe about the Bible?

g According to Baptist belief, who may be baptized?

h What does 'going right under the water' symbolize?

i Give some reasons why you agree or disagree with the Baptist policy of only baptizing people who really believe in Jesus.

5 Discuss

Do you think that Christians need a special building to worship in?

New initiatives

In recent years many Christians have started to meet again in houses to worship God. We call these '**House Churches**'. They are a growing influence in the Church today.

THE HOUSEHOLD OF FAITH

St Paul called the Church the 'household of faith'. He told people to do good to everybody, and especially to those who belong to the household of faith.

In the New Testament, the church is often referred to as a house or household.

In those days, of course, there were no church buildings and the church met at someone's house. There was a church in Rome which met at the house of Priscilla and Aquila (Romans 16:5) and one in Corinth which met at the house of Chloe (I Corinthians 1:11).

Throughout Christian history there have always been attempts to get closer to what the Bible actually wants people to do. This is why John Wesley and William Booth took the stand they did in trying to help the poor. They wanted everyone to know about Jesus and the way Christianity can change people's lives.

The Baptists wanted to be more consistent with what they thought the New Testament was really saying about baptism.

Later, the Brethren believed very strongly that it was wrong to have a paid ministry. If St Paul could go on being a tentmaker, then there was no need to have special people paid to tell others about Jesus.

D House Church worship

6 Look at Acts 4:32–35.

a Make a list of the things which made the Christian community in Jerusalem different from other people at the time.

b Which ideals from this list do you think that members of the house churches might try to put into practice?

c Do you think that these ideals are the kind of things which Jesus meant his followers to do?

d Is there any way in which this seems different from the other churches you have studied?

Dependence on Bible and Holy Spirit.	Shared experience of God.	HOUSE CHURCHES	Gospel affects every part of life.
Close relationships.	Everyone shares decisions.	Commitment to each other.	Every member has a function.
JESUS IS THE FOUNDATION			

e You might like to draw a similar diagram putting in the different bricks in the structure of another church which you have studied. Or are the bricks actually the same? What do you think?

'THAT THEY MAY BE ONE'

Many Christians want to have closer links with other Churches. They believe that it is wrong for Christians to be separated from one another.

On the night before he died, Jesus prayed that his followers would be united. ''That they may be one, as you and I are one, Father.'' He said that the way Christians could be identified would be by the way they loved one another.

Sadly, over the years, there have been divisions between Christians which have caused hurt and bloodshed. The world's 1105 million Christians are still divided into 659 million Roman Catholics, 123 million Orthodox, and 323 million Protestants (1988 figures).

MISSIONARY WORK OVERLAPS

As **missionaries** began to tell people about Jesus in the nineteenth century, they also began to draw new Christians into their own **denominations**, so the divisions which originated in Europe and the Near East were exported. Sometimes the missionary work of different Churches

B World Council of Churches in session

has overlapped, and so developing nations have heard varying versions of the **Gospel**.

POINTING THE WAY TOWARDS UNITY

It was the missionaries who first began to point the way towards unity. The Missionary Conference in Edinburgh in 1910 began to make moves towards a closer association between the Churches. By 1948, the need to draw closer

together had been made clearer in the aftermath of the war, and the **World Council of Churches** (WCC) was formed. Today, there are more than 300 member Churches of the World Council of Churches.

VISITS BY CHURCH LEADERS

Another step forward came in 1960 when Dr Geoffrey Fisher, who was Archbishop of Canterbury, visited Pope

A South American missionaries

C Pope John Paul II with the Archbishop of Canterbury

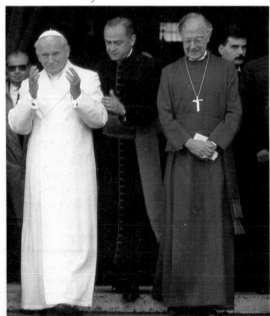

John XXIII. This was the start of more open relationships between the Roman Catholic Church and other Churches.

VATICAN II

In January 1959, Pope John XXIII decided to call a great council called the Second Vatican Council. Sessions were held in Rome from 1960 to 1965, and observers were invited from other denominations as well as from the Roman Catholic Church all over the world. For the first time, Pope John allowed the services of the Church to be in local languages instead of in Latin.

There is a new enthusiasm for unity within the whole Church. Ordinary Christians are now taking a much greater part in Church affairs and are much better informed about their faith. Consequently, they want to remove some of the barriers between Churches.

LOOKING AT SIMILARITIES INSTEAD OF DIFFERENCES

The differences have centred around:

a what people believe about baptism

b the way the Churches celebrate Holy Communion (Eucharist)

c the different kinds of clergy (ministry).

In the past most of the thinking centred around the things which divided the Churches. Now people are trying to concentrate on the things which they have in common. In many ways the Churches are now trying to work together, on projects helping famine relief, Third World education, self help schemes in developing countries, etc. More and more Christians are discovering the unity they already have with one another, simply because they all acknowledge Jesus Christ as their Lord.

NOTES/DATABASE

Use the glossary to look up the meanings of the following words. Then use the definitions to make your own notes or suitable entries on your database.

Missionaries   World Council of Churches

Denomination

Gospel   Ecumenical

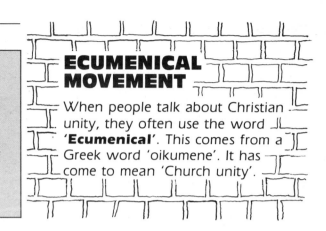

ECUMENICAL MOVEMENT

When people talk about Christian unity, they often use the word **'Ecumenical'**. This comes from a Greek word 'oikumene'. It has come to mean 'Church unity'.

ACTIVITIES

1 Quick quiz

a How do Christians know that Jesus wanted his followers to be united?

b Design a bar chart showing the numbers of Christians in the three major divisions.

c Why do you think that missionaries became concerned about Christian unity?

d What was the first step towards unity?

e When was the World Council of Churches begun?

f Why was the visit to the Pope by the Archbishop of Canterbury important?

g What difference has Vatican II made?

h List the three major areas of difference.

i What change in attitude has there been in recent years?

2 What can we learn from the Bible?

"There is no difference between Jew and Gentile, between slaves and freemen, between men and women. You are all united because you believe in Jesus Christ."
(Galatians 3:28)

Read I Corinthians 1:10–17.

"Agree in everything you say so that there won't be any divisions among you."

a Do you think Paul was upset about the divisions in the Church at Corinth?

b What was the argument all about?

c What kinds of differences of opinion are there in the Church now?

d What advice do you think that Paul would give to Christians now about their differences of opinion?

FURTHER ACTIVITIES

WORKING TOGETHER: THE WORLD COUNCIL OF CHURCHES

For many years, some Christians have wanted to try to get rid of the divisions in the Church. In 1948, the World Council of Churches met for the first time. They chose Geneva in Switzerland to be the headquarters because Switzerland is a neutral country and many other world organizations such as the World Health Organization already have their headquarters there.

Over 300 different Churches are members of the WCC. They include many of the old established churches such as the Anglican Church and the Methodist Church, as well as many of the newer churches.

Although the Roman Catholic Church is not a member of the WCC, it always sends representatives, and joins in projects to help developing countries.

1 Using the information on the diagram of the World Council of Churches, copy and complete the following chart:

Work of World Council of Churches

Faith	Education	Justice

2 How do you think that working together in the ways shown in your chart might help Christians to

a understand more about one another?

b become more united?

c show the world what being a Christian really means?

LOCAL COUNCILS OF CHURCHES

3 Many areas have their own local Council of Churches.

Find out . . .

a whether there is one in your area

b which are the member churches

c what kind of things it discusses

d what it does

e what events it has organized.

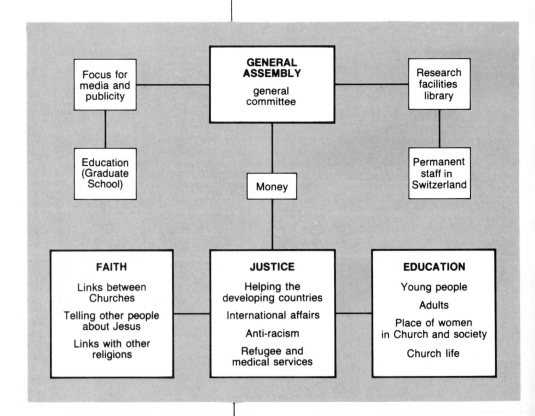

TAIZÉ

For many people the name Taizé has come to symbolize unity.

Look at the map below to see the location of Taizé.

There is also a picture of the Prior of Taizé, Roger Schultz.

He first came to Taizé in 1940, but had to leave because he was hiding Jewish people. After the war he returned and began the religious community at Taizé. The brothers at Taizé are from all the different Churches, and from many nations. They share a common life in which no one has any personal possessions and everyone works together in a self-sufficient community. Worship, and especially the Eucharist, are at the centre of their lives.

In the 1960s young people started to come to Taizé to share in the life of the brothers. They usually stay for a week on the vast campsite and join in the worship. Many groups from English churches go to Taizé to discover together more about being a Christian.

"The music is at the heart of it."

The simple but majestic music of Taizé affects people very deeply as they seek to find out more about God during their time at Taizé.

"No one ever asks whether you are a Catholic or a Baptist, or even if you are a believer at all."

(. . . a visitor)

"We do not seek to convert, it's only God who does that."

(. . . Brother Paul)

4 Imagine you are from an English church.

Write a letter home to your friends telling them about the life at Taizé.

5 **Something to think about**

a Why do you think 3000 young people a week visit Taizé each summer?

b Do you think that Taizé's emphasis on unity and peace can help young people understand more about being a Christian in today's world?

c Look at Acts 2:42–47, 4:32–35, and Galatians 3:28. How far do you think that the life at Taizé fits in with the picture of Christian life in these quotations?

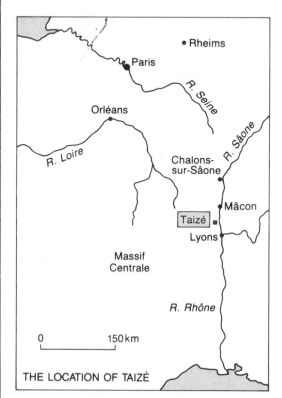

THE LOCATION OF TAIZÉ

D Brother Roger

E The campsite at Taizé

Abba Hebrew word for father

Adam The Hebrew word for 'man'

Altar A special place to worship God

Anglican A name for the group of Churches linked with the Church of England

Anointed Kings are anointed at their coronation

Apocrypha Jewish holy books which are not normally included in the Old Testament. (That is, excluded from the Canon of Scripture at the Council of Jamnia.)

Apostle Someone sent out with a special message

Aramaic The everyday language which Jesus spoke

Archbishop A chief bishop

Baptize Using water as a sign that someone has become a follower of Jesus

Bar Mitzvah The ceremony in which a Jewish boy takes the responsibility of manhood

Bedouin Tribe of wandering herdsmen who live in tents

Believer The New Testament uses the word believer to mean Christian

Bishop A church leader in charge of a geographical area

Blasphemy Speaking against God

Canaan The land which the Israelites settled in when they left Egypt

Cardinal A leader of the Roman Catholic Church with responsibility for electing the Pope

Church A group of people who meet together to worship Jesus

Codex An early form of book

Confirmation The second half of baptism, in which a person takes for themselves promises made at their baptism

Covenant An agreement between two or more people

Creed A belief, or list of beliefs

Crucifixion Method of execution used by the Romans of nailing someone to a cross

Curate An assistant to a vicar

Deacon The first 'order' in which someone is ordained

Dead Sea Scrolls A collection of scrolls from the time of Jesus and earlier found near the Dead Sea

Delegate Someone who attends a meeting or conference representing others

Denomination An individual Christian church eg Methodist

Diocese A geographical area looked after by a bishop

Disciple A person who follows and learns from someone else

Ecumenical A movement towards Church unity

Edict of Milan The law which made Christianity legal in the Roman Empire

Emperor The leader of the Romans

Epistle A letter in the New Testament

Eucharist A name for the service which commemorates the Last Supper

Exodus The time when the Israelites left Egypt and entered the Promised Land

Font A special container for the water for baptism

Fourth Gospel The Gospel written by John, Jesus' disciple

Fresco Wall painting.

Gentile A person who is not a Jew

Gospel Word meaning 'good news', usually good news about Jesus

Great Schism The division of the church between East and West

Holy Communion Service which remembers Jesus' last supper with the disciples. Also called Eucharist or Mass

Ikon Religious painting on wood

Immersion The act of going right under the surface of the water during baptism

Incense A substance burned during some church services

Islam Religion of people who follow Mohammed

Jew Descendant of Abraham

Judasim The belief of the Jews

Laity Ordinary Church members who are not ordained

Law The Law was a set of rules to help Jews serve God

Manuscript Hand written document

Mass Catholic name for service celebrating the Last Supper

Messiah The person expected by the Jews to help them and lead them. The word 'Messiah' is Hebrew for 'anointed'

Ministry The time when Jesus was showing the people who he was and telling them about God

Missionaries People who have the job of telling others about Jesus

Monastery Place where monks live

Monk A person who lives a life dedicated to God, usually in a monastery

Monotheistic Believing in one God only

Muslim Follower of Mohammed

Nicene Creed A list of Christian beliefs drawn up at the Council of Nicea

Ordained Someone is ordained when he or she is made a deacon, priest or bishop

Orthodox Group of Christian Churches found mainly in Eastern Europe and the Eastern Mediterranean

Papyrus Surface for writing made from reeds

Paraclete Name used for Holy Spirit in John's Gospel

Parish Area which is looked after by a vicar or parish priest

Passover Jewish festival remembering the escape of the Israelites from Egypt

Patriarch Chief bishop in the Orthodox Church

Penance A sign of God's forgiveness

Penance box The place where a Roman Catholic receives forgiveness of sins

Pentateuch The first five books in the Old Testament

Pentecost i Jewish festival recalling the gift of the Ten Commandments ii Christian festival recalling the gift of the Holy Spirit

Persecuted Being mistreated, imprisoned or tortured because of beliefs

Pilgrimage A journey with a religious purpose

Polytheistic Believing in more than one god

Pope Leader of the Roman Catholic Church

Promised Land The land which God promised to Abraham (Genesis 12:4)

Prophecy Words spoken by a prophet

Prophet People who explain the Word of God for their times

Protestant Churches which are not Roman Catholic or Orthodox

Qumran The place where the Dead Sea Scrolls were found

Rabbi Jewish religious leader

Reader A lay person who is trained to preach and take services

Reformation Sixteenth century movement for changing the church

Resurrection Returning to life after death, especially as applied to Jesus

Revealed Teaching about a God who wants to make himself known to people

Roman Empire The area ruled by the Romans

Rosary A set of beads counted to help people recite a series of prayers

Sacrament An act of worship with a deeper meaning

Scriptures Literally 'writings', usually the Bible

Scroll Rolled papyrus on which the Bible was first written

Septuagint Greek translation of Old Testament

Sermon A talk to help people to understand more about the Christian faith

Shrine A special place to worship God

Slava bread Yugoslavian food for religious festivals

Synagogue Place where Jews worship

Synoptic Gospels Matthew, Mark, Luke.

Ten Commandments The rules which God gave the Israelites

Vatican The centre of government of the Roman Catholic Church

Vellum Surface for writing made from calf skin

Vestry A dressing room for the choir and the clergy

Vicar An Anglican clergyman in charge of a parish

World Council of Churches An organization linking over 300 churches

Ziggurat A temple for moon worship